Penguin Handbooks
Town Gardens to Live In

Susan Jellicoe was educated at St Paul's Girls' School, Hammersmith, and the Sorbonne, Paris. In 1936 she married a landscape architect, Geoffrey Jellicoe, with whom she has visited gardens all over the world. She designs planting schemes in her husband's office and has collaborated with him on three books, *Modern Private Gardens* (1968), *Water: The Use of Water in Landscape Architecture* (1971) and *The Landscape of Man* (1975). As well as collaborating with Lady Allen on two previous books, she is part author of *The Gardens of Mughul India* (1972). From 1961 to 1965 Mrs Jellicoe edited the *Observer*'s Gardening Panel. She is an Honorary Associate of the Institute of Landscape Architects.

Marjory Allen was born in 1897 and married Clifford Allen, later Lord Allen of Hurtwood, in 1921. They had one daughter. Educated at Bedales School and Reading University, Lady Allen became a landscape architect, specializing in roof gardens and playgrounds. She helped to found the Institute of Landscape Architects, of which she was a Fellow, and a Vice-President from 1939 to 1946. She was also Chairman of the Coronation Planting Committee from 1937 to 1939. For fifteen years she was gardening correspondent of the *Manchester Guardian*. Among her many publications are *Things We See: Gardens* (1953) and *The New Small Garden* (1956), both with Susan Jellicoe. Her *Memoirs of an Uneducated Lady* (1975) appeared shortly before her death in 1976.

# *Town Gardens to Live In*

*Susan Jellicoe and Marjory Allen*

*Penguin Books*

Penguin Books Ltd, Harmondsworth,
Middlesex, England
Penguin Books, 625 Madison Avenue, New York,
New York 10022, U.S.A.
Penguin Books Australia Ltd, Ringwood,
Victoria, Australia
Penguin Books Canada Ltd, 2801 John Street,
Markham, Ontario, Canada L3R 1B4
Penguin Books (N.Z.) Ltd, 182-190 Wairau Road,
Auckland 10, New Zealand

First published 1977

Copyright © Susan Jellicoe and Marjory Allen, 1977
All rights reserved

Printed in Great Britain by
Fletcher & Sons Ltd, Norwich
Set in Monotype Plantin

Except in the United States of America,
this book is sold subject to the condition that
it shall not, by way of trade or otherwise, be lent,
re-sold, hired out, or otherwise circulated without
the publisher's prior consent in any form of
binding or cover other than that in which it is
published and without a similar condition
including this condition being imposed on the
subsequent purchaser

## Contents

Acknowledgements 7
Introduction 9
1. The bones of design 14
2. Six gardens 33
3. Creating an illusion 46
4. The garden floor 55
5. Walls and screens 68
6. Water 77
7. Shade and winter 90
8. Planning for easy maintenance 101
9. Sitting space 107
10. Children 116
11. Eats 122
12. The naturalist 130
13. Roof gardens 136
14. Pots and containers 144
15. Front gardens 154
16. Utilities 161
Appendix 1: Construction notes 165
*Brick retaining walls – Plastic pools – Concrete – Imperial and metric measures*
Appendix 2: Finding out 180
Index 185

# *Acknowledgements*

Our first thanks must go to the many owners who allowed us to visit their gardens and answered our questions. In each case we learned something of value, although some gardens had later to be omitted for lack of space. We should also like to thank the Islington Gardeners, the Royal Society for the Protection of Birds and Miss Nicolette Franck of the Cement and Concrete Association for their help, and Miss Brenda Colvin for advice on Chapter 14.

For their generosity in providing plans and photographs, we are greatly indebted to the following designers:

DESIGNERS

Robert Adams, pl. 54; Sidney Arrobus, pl. 126, fig. 24; W. J. Boer, pl. 49; Patricia and Kenneth Booth, pl. 30; John Brookes, pls. 2 (with Lady Allen), 4, 9, 12, 13–17, 50, 58, 60 and 80 (with Cyril Fradan), 91, 92, 94, 119–20, 130 (with Philip Pank), 155, 161, figs. 3, 8, 10, 11; Andreas Bruun, pl. 143, fig. 27; Peter Coats, pl. 71; Timothy Cochrane, pls. 47, 159, fig. 4; Lester Collins, pls. 65, 105; P. Gadd Collins, pls. 128–9, figs. 25–6; Brenda Colvin pls. 32, 61, 102, 133; Dame Sylvia Crowe, pl. 39; Anne Dudley-Ward, pls. 103–4; Cyril Fradan (with John Brookes), pls. 60, 80; Sir Frederick Gibberd, fig. 5; Greater London Town Development Division/John Talbot, pls. 19–20, fig. 13; Allan Hart, pl. 144; Arne Jacobsen, pl. 52; Geoffrey Jellicoe, pls. 27, 36, 64, 69, 70 (with Lanning Roper), 87; John King, pls. 141–2; Olaf Klaaborg of the Gruppen for landskabsplanlaegning A/S, pls. 74, 83; Morten Klint, fig. 6; Graham Lang, pl. 56; Eywin Langkilde, pls. 41, 99; Hans Luz, pls. 10, 11, 127, fig. 9; Frederick McManus, pls. 6–8, fig. 7; Leonard Manasseh, pls. 106–7; Milton Keynes Development Corporation, pls. 44, 46, 97, 151; Barbara Oakley, pls. 95, 145; A. du Gard Pasley, pls. 18, 42, 43, 59, 62, 63, figs. 12, 17, 19; Gordon Patterson, pl. 35; P. Powell, pl. 84; Alan Reiach, pl. 57; Sir Gordon Russell, pl. 88;

Richard Schreiner, p. 9; Graham Shankland, pl. 48; Geoffrey Smith, p. 10, pl. 34; Tony Southard, pl. 33, fig. 18; David Stevens, pls. 28, 101, fig. 16; Ann Stokes, pl. 115; Tayler & Green, pls. 81, 125; Noel Tweddell, pls. 26, 77; Max Thoma, pl. 67; Felix Walter, fig. 21; Rosemary Wren and Peter Crotty, pl. 122; Monica Young, pls. 139-40; G. P. Youngman, pl. 86.

PHOTOGRAPHS

Joseph Alsop, pl. 72; W. J. Boer, pl. 49; John Brookes, pls. 2, 4, 9, 50, 58, 63, 92, 94; Andreas Bruun, pl. 143; Cement and Concrete Association, pls. 39, 163-7, fig. 30; Lester Collins, pls. 65, 105; P. Gadd Collins, pls. 128-9; Brenda Colvin, pl. 32; Cyril Fradan, pl. 80; L. Goldman, pl. 117; Greater London Council, pls. 19-20; Gruppen for landskabsplanlaegning A/S, pls. 74, 83; Allan Hart, pl. 144; R. Hyne, pl. 122; Arne Jacobsen, pl. 52; Graham Lang, pl. 56; Eywin Langkilde, pls. 41, 99; Maurice Lee, pl. 37; Hans Luz, pls. 10-11, 127; Frederick McManus, pls. 6-8; Milton Keynes Development Corporation, pls. 44, 46, 97, 151; Mono Concrete, pls. 53, 138, 154; Gordon Patterson, pl. 35; George Perkin, pl. 88; Alan Reiach, pl. 57; Richard Schreiner, p. 9; Graham Shankland, pl. 48; Elizabeth Simson, pl. 123; Geoffrey Smith, p. 10, pl. 34; Tony Southard, pl. 33; David Stevens, pls. 28, 101; Tayler & Green, pls. 81, 125; Max Thoma, pl. 67; Monica Young, pls. 139-40.

All photographs not otherwise credited are by Susan Jellicoe

# Introduction

This book is about your garden as part of your living space. Its purpose is to help you make the most of your particular plot by suggesting solutions to some of the special problems of town gardens and ways in which you could adapt the space to suit your needs. It contains detailed advice on the selection and arrangement of plants, but does not tell you a great deal about how to grow them. There are already many excellent books on every aspect of horticulture and the day-to-day care of plants.

The first few chapters deal with design in general and the relationship between design and use. They are followed by chapters on specific problems and how to meet the many and varied demands that may be made on a garden because of the owner's interests and tastes or because of its situation. To find a complete answer to a problem, therefore, you may have to consult more than one chapter. Construction notes at the end of the book give guidance on simple structural operations like laying paving and making small pools. You may, however, think it worth while to buy a good do-it-yourself manual. One of the most comprehensive, the *Reader's Digest Complete Do-it-yourself Manual* (costing £8·50 in 1976), would be a good investment if major structural operations are planned. And you would be wise to get one of the general nurserymen's catalogues listed on pp. 182–3.

Introduction

The gardens which give the most pleasure to their owners have generally been thought out in advance. People are sometimes put off by the word 'design', which they think of as being solely the concern of specialists. But we all make design choices nearly every day (clothes, furnishings, even meals) and may have to live with our mistakes for years if we don't give ourselves time to think and make use of our sense of good proportion. On a simple rectangular plot, it is not difficult to plan a garden once you have taken stock of the possibilities and decided how it is to be used, both now and in the future; a plan should be capable of adaptation, particularly where there are children. It can be carried out in stages and there is much to be said for letting a garden develop gradually, once the basic lines have been settled.

If your garden is an awkward shape or presents other difficulties, you might consider paying a professional designer to make an overall plan which you can carry out yourself at your leisure (see p. 183). The cost of this is offset in two ways: first, you are less

## Town Gardens to Live In

likely to waste time and money on mistakes; second, you will be gaining valuable living space at much less than the cost of building an extra room. You can reduce the cost by making your own survey as described on p. 24. A lot depends on how long you expect to live in the same house, and this is one of the first questions you should ask yourself before planning an expensive programme of works.

A town garden can be a green oasis among the bricks and mortar, with a secluded place to sit, somewhere for children's play and as many plants as can conveniently be squeezed in, even on the tops of walls. It brings us, if briefly, into contact with nature. This too can be planned for: leaves brushing lightly against us as we walk along a path, the scent of flowers as we sit watching the bees at work or listening to the splash of a small fountain, the sound of birds settling down for the night or the rustle of wind in the leaves, a tomato still warm from the sun or a handful of alpine strawberries grown as ground cover.

Flowers are the most obvious of the garden's visual pleasures.

Introduction

Others are incidental or can be contrived – a tree planted where the tracery of its branches is seen against the sky, a framed glimpse of the garden seen from the windows of the house, a shrub with sunlight from behind lighting up the leaves, or the quivering shadows of leaves on paving. Gardens present a constantly changing spectacle, varying from hour to hour, from season to season and year to year.

The gardens illustrated in this book range from small paved courtyards in city centres to gardens in the suburbs and on housing estates. They are not shown as models to be copied, but as a source of stimulating ideas. The problems facing their owners are similar – mainly lack of privacy and shortage of space. But no two gardens are exactly alike. You, as a gardener, must find your own answers. In doing so you will, with luck, create a garden which not only suits your needs but expresses your personality. As the sculptor Eric Gill wrote: 'An artist is not a special kind of man. Every man is a special kind of artist.'

# 1  The Bones of Design

When making or altering a garden, it is tempting to fly into immediate action. Resist the temptation firmly. It is better to risk losing a growing season by taking time to work out a satisfactory plan than to be forced to make difficult adjustments later on. So let action be confined to sowing a few annuals while you sit back and assess the possibilities.

## ASSESSING YOUR PLOT

The first step is to find out about the garden itself: the type of soil, which influences what can be grown there; whether there is too

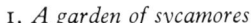
1. *A garden of sycamores*

## The Bones of Design

little or too much movement of air, and the prevailing direction of the wind; what trees there are, casting shadows and perhaps impoverishing the soil; what dank corners where frost can do most damage; which way the garden faces in relation to the sun, and thus where and when the garden will be in shadow.

A look at the plants in neighbouring gardens will tell you a great deal about the soil (if they are sickly and yellow-looking, the soil is poor and lacks nitrogen; flourishing rhododendrons and azaleas indicate absence of lime; roses do well on clay and are tolerant of chalk; and so on). In some town gardens, builders' rubbish is buried not far below the surface. Unless you are prepared to spend a lot of money or several years in getting rid of it and building up the soil, stick to plants that thrive almost anywhere, or even follow the example of the owner of the garden in pl. 1: having looked at the struggling plants in his neighbours' gardens, he decided to make the best of the sycamore saplings that almost covered his site and cut them to create a vista.

Wind will soon make its presence felt and can be diverted or diminished by a hedge, fence or other barrier. Poor air circulation is a more difficult problem, but it can sometimes be improved by removing obstacles, such as heavy blocks of planting, or thinning out hedges. Any decision about the trees (whether too many or few) should be left until a plan has been worked out (see p. 24).

The sun is a difficult factor to assess, because the shadows that it casts change from hour to hour and from day to day throughout the year. Just how much these can vary is shown by two drawings overleaf. One shows the shadows in early spring and autumn at three different times of day; the other, the changes in summer. Until you know how this applies to your garden, your planning will be on a hit or miss basis. For example, it is obviously convenient for a child's sand-pit, a terrace or a herb bed to be near the house, but neither the child, nor you, nor the plants, will be very happy if the sun barely reaches the spot. And there is little point in planting spring crocuses in a part of the garden that is in shadow until the end of March, however sunny it may be in summer, for it is the sun's rays that make the flowers open out.

Sloping ground is another point to be considered at this stage.

# Town Gardens to Live In

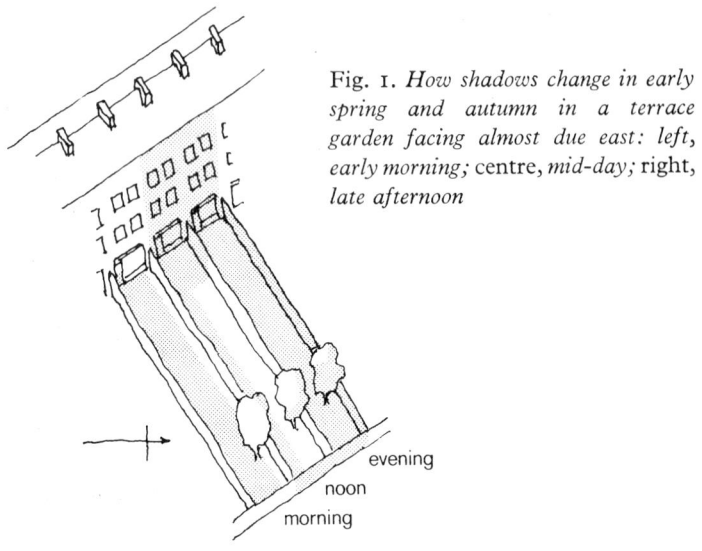

Fig. 1. *How shadows change in early spring and autumn in a terrace garden facing almost due east:* left, *early morning;* centre, *mid-day;* right, *late afternoon*

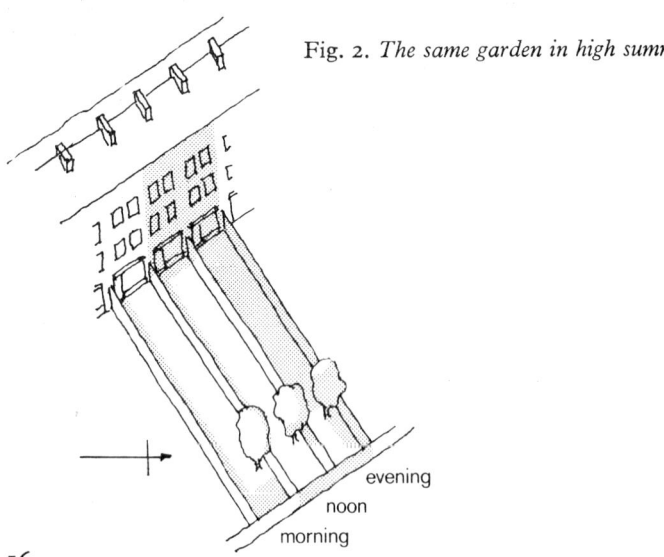

Fig. 2. *The same garden in high summer*

# The Bones of Design

Unless the slope is very gradual, it may be better to level it into shallow terraces (see pl. 12) which are more useful as living space or for planting and very suitable in a formal or architectural garden. The first step is to remove the topsoil from the whole area to be worked to a depth of six inches, and put it on one side until it can be re-spread. This is especially important if the terraces are to be grassed or planted: grass needs six inches of topsoil, herbaceous perennials twelve inches, shrubs eighteen inches. You should not take from the lower level more subsoil than can conveniently be spread on the upper level. Terraces are also an excellent way to dispose of rubbish and rubble, but be sure to remove the topsoil from the area where you are going to put the rubbish.

Finally, should the immediate surroundings be blocked out or brought into the design? Nearly all town gardens are overlooked by the neighbouring houses. It is impossible to protect the whole garden from view, but one corner can usually be found which with a little ingenuity can be converted into a secluded oasis. On the other hand, a fine tree in the next garden or an architectural feature such as a church spire (pl. 2) can provide a focal point and an extra dimension.

*2. The church spire plays an important part in the design of this London garden*

Town Gardens to Live In

The elements that must be fitted into the space at your disposal will depend on how you are going to use the garden; there might be a sitting-out place, provision for children's play, flower beds or vegetable patch, plus a small working area for compost and a tool shed – an essential in all but the smallest gardens – and arrangements for dustbins and other household needs. Some of these will be competing for the sunniest spot or that nearest the house, so it is important to decide which has first claim. Access in all weathers must be provided: a path to the working area, for example, or to dustbins outside the back gate. These are the factors that control where the paved areas are to be, and how large.

## WHAT KIND OF GARDEN?

The overall character of a town garden is determined by two basic design principles: it is either an extension of the rooms of the house

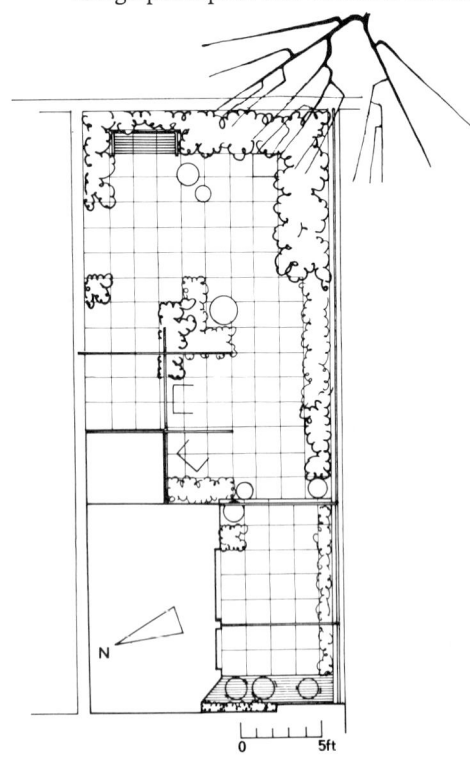

Fig. 3. *Plan of a garden that is an extension of the house*

# The Bones of Design

Fig. 4. *Plan of a garden based on an illusion of the country come to town. Occasional blocks of planting at each side of the garden make it impossible to see from one end to the other*

(fig. 3), or an illusion of country come to town (fig. 4). Many gardens contain elements of both, but to be successful, one kind of design should dominate. Personal inclination – the pull towards formality or romanticism – will be the deciding factor, modified by the requirements of daily use.

One striking difference between the two types of garden is the way the boundaries are handled. Where the garden is treated as an outdoor room, these are clearly seen and the shape of the enclosure

3. The country comes to town in north London

4. An outdoor room that is an extension of the house

## The Bones of Design

is important, though this should not mean that the whole garden can be taken in at a glance. The floor pattern is also prominent. And since this type of design is based on geometry, one way of arriving at an overall sense of harmony is to relate the measurements of all spaces and structures to the dimensions of whatever paving slab has been chosen. This is similar to the Japanese *tatami* system, where the standard size of the small mats covering the floor of a house is the basis of the proportions of all the other elements of the structure. It is the method used in the plan in fig. 3, where the position of the pergola and the breaking up of the space has been worked out in multiples of the paving slabs. Pursued to an extreme, the results can be boring; fortunately, every garden has irregularities that cause slight variations which, with the help of the planting, prevent monotony.

The success of the country-style garden depends almost entirely on concealing the boundaries and using loose, informal planting, rather than screens or hedges, to create separate compartments within the garden. This is not, however, a natural garden, but one where nature is under strict control ('organized woodland' is one owner's description of her north London garden). To be effective, the vegetation should be on a fairly bold scale, but a constant watch is necessary to prevent the garden from turning into an impenetrable jungle – concealed order as opposed to the more obvious order of the outdoor room.

Whether you settle for romanticism or geometry, or a combination of both, one further general point should be borne in mind. This is the question of scale: the furnishings of the garden – trees, shrubs, sculpture, etc. – should not dwarf the house or garden, nor should they be so small as to look insignificant. This chiefly affects the choice of plants and is dealt with on pp. 25–7.

## MAKING A PLAN

All the information you have collected and all the decisions you have taken must now be put together to make an arrangement of spaces that is pleasant to live in and satisfies your needs. No one should feel bashful about launching into the field of design. After all, every garden owner is an expert on his plot and his needs, and he can look forward to the satisfaction of creating a garden that is an expression of his own personality and is therefore unique. It may contain traces of ideas gathered from different sources, but these will have been transformed by the needs of the site into something more than a straight copy.

It is obviously impossible to condense into a few paragraphs the wisdom that a professional designer gains in years of training and experience. Nevertheless, here are a few general guide-lines.

Keep the broad lines of the design as simple as possible, or you may end up with oddly shaped spaces that are difficult to maintain and have no real use. Complicated details that are difficult to carry out may look amateurish and are probably best left alone. Plants and people will in any case provide plenty of interest.

In dividing the total area into compartments for different kinds of use, try not to make them equal in size, or your design will be indeterminate and confused as to its purpose. Taking a more positive line (which is also more restful), a garden with roughly one third devoted to a sitting area and the rest to planting is clearly a green garden with somewhere to sit, whereas a very small garden almost entirely taken up by the sitting space is predominantly a paved garden with some plants.

A very long narrow garden might be broken up into three or four compartments of varying lengths, according to the purpose for which they are intended. Similar principles about proportion should be applied to any decision about the ground pattern, discussed in detail on p. 56.

A pathway is the backbone of the design of all but the smallest *formal* gardens and should be integrated with the sitting area and other elements which it links. In large gardens, paths are usually wide enough for two people to walk side by side; in a small garden the width required by a person with a wheelbarrow is more in keeping with the scale of the garden. If the path has to cross from one side of the plot to the other, it should do so without cutting across any of the spaces at random (see fig. 5). A path is a very strong feature in a garden and if it cannot be related to the basic design of spaces it should pass through them as inconspicuously as

# The Bones of Design

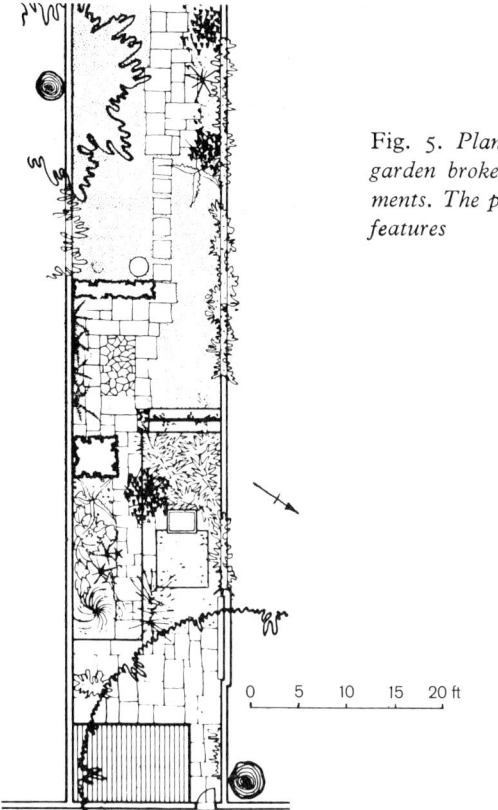

Fig. 5. *Plan of a long narrow garden broken up into compartments. The path is related to the features*

possible. Examples of 'muted' paths are: stepping-stones, paths slightly sunk below grass level or hard-surface paths that have been made green by grass or moss growing between the joints. A path that winds for no apparent reason may become irritating in time; a tree or large shrub planted inside the bend will make the curve seem inevitable.

In semi-wild *informal* gardens, paths play a less prominent part in the design and should be minimal: perhaps large stepping-stones set into the grass with four to five inches between, to allow the grass to flow through. They may even be dispensed with altogether if the grass is wide enough to vary the route to the end of the garden. A more solid path of closely set stones or bricks can be made to cross a lawn almost invisibly if it is sunk slightly below the level of the turf. In this case, it is better to leave the joints unmortared, to allow rainwater to seep away.

In planning a garden, many gardeners rely a good deal, and rightly, on their intuition. But it can be helpful to clarify one's ideas by drawing a plan on paper, particularly if it is to be carried out in stages. Work at a scale of $\frac{1}{8}$ inch to a foot (i.e. 1 in. represents 8 ft) for most gardens, or $\frac{1}{4}$ inch to a foot for very small gardens.

If the plot is not too complicated by irregular boundaries, changes of level, oddly placed trees, etc., you can make your own rough survey, using the following procedure: (*a*) make a rough sketch of the outline of the plot in a notebook; (*b*) mark what measurements are essential; (*c*) pace these as accurately as possible, which you can do after determining the length of your stride, or use a tape-measure; (*d*) re-draw the site plan to scale. In a small rectangular garden the whole operation should take less than an hour.

Having now got the outline of the plot on paper it is possible to superimpose tracing paper on which suggestions can be roughed in; if not satisfactory, the tracing paper can be put on one side and a fresh piece substituted. When the design seems about to jell, you can block out in appropriate colours the different areas – grass, planting beds, sitting space, paths, etc. Another method is to cut out pieces of paper, coloured and shaped to represent the various elements, and pin them to the outline drawing, moving them round until a satisfactory arrangement is reached. Finally, turn the completed plan upside down and look at it as a piece of abstract design. If the shape still pleases you, mark it out on the ground with pegs and see if it works in practice and if adjustments are needed.

Irregularly shaped plots are more difficult to handle. It may be best simply to mark out paths, paved areas, etc., on the ground with wooden pegs. On a triangular site, such as fig. 6, blocks of planting should be planned to create spaces that are a more convenient shape and pleasant to sit in.

# The Bones of Design

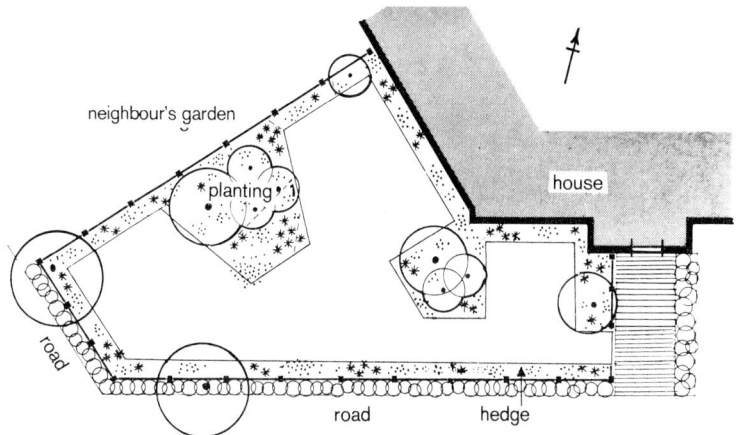

Fig. 6. *Plan of a triangular garden*

## PLANTING

### Trees

Accepting the existing conditions for growth is the first essential for successful planting, but finding the right scale comes a close second. Begin with the largest unit, the tree, for which room should be found in all but the smallest courtyard gardens – and sometimes even there, if it can be placed close to a wall. The height and spread should be related to the size of the garden, and here the suburban gardener is fortunate, for there are any number of medium-sized ornamental trees and a few medium-sized forest trees, such as the rowan (*Sorbus aucuparia*), birch (*Betula*) and wild gean or bird cherry (*Prunus avium*).

For the small garden, a slender form of growth and delicate foliage that does not rob the garden or house of light are more important than height (which in general should not exceed twenty-five feet). Small cherries like *Prunus serrula* (pl. 5); three sophisticated members of the rowan family, *Sorbus vilmorinii*, *S. hupehensis* and *S. discolor*; a drooping birch (*Betula pendula* Dalecarlica); all these are suitable. If you have more room, you could choose a tree with a wider spread, such as the golden acacia (*Robinia pseudoacacia*

25

5. Prunus serrula: *the right height for a small garden*

Frisia), the winter-flowering cherry (*Prunus subhirtella* Autumnalis) and a twisted version of the Pekin willow (*Salix matsudana* Tortuosa). Fastigiate trees, whose branches grow upwards instead of sideways, are also suitable for small gardens if used sparingly. They take little ground space yet give an air of solid form and maturity. Hornbeam, hawthorn, juniper, cherry and crab apple all have upward-growing varieties. The choice of tree and its position on plan partly depend on whether it is to give privacy, to hide an eyesore, to break up the line of a wall or to give a sense of depth by introducing an object (the tree trunk) round which the garden seems to be in movement.

Should pruning become necessary (perhaps because you have taken over a garden with a large tree), take advice from your local Council or nearest nursery, who will recommend an expert tree surgeon. For small trees and shrubs, consult one of the many good books on pruning.

The Bones of Design

If a tree is directly associated with shrubs or herbaceous plants, the overall balance or composition of the planting bed should be studied. Decide, first, the position of the tree, then the larger shrubs and finally the herbaceous plants and ground cover. These last can easily be rearranged, but trees do not take kindly to being uprooted and the disturbance is far greater. If possible, the tree should not come between the other plants and the sun, unless you are going to use plants that will tolerate the shade.

*Shrubs and herbaceous perennials*

A mixed bed of shrubs and herbaceous plants is particularly suitable for a small garden. In a limited space, it is difficult to keep up a succession of colourful flowers, and too much colour can in any case be restful. Form becomes more important. A loosely arranged backbone of shrubs gives substance to the planting – in winter too, if they are evergreen – and acts as a setting for smaller groups of flowers as and when they blossom. The size of the shrubs should be related to the size of the garden. To show off their shape, they should be allowed enough room to grow to their full size without crowding out the human occupants; nothing is sadder than a tree or shrub that has been crippled by drastic pruning. Clues to the ultimate size of most shrubs in general use can be found in the catalogues of some of the larger nurseries (see p. 182). The empty space which will eventually be taken up by the shrub can be filled with herbaceous or ground-cover plants that can be disposed of later without too great a pang.

The shrubs will be seen to much better effect if they are not all massed at the back or in the middle. Place one or two near the front and allow them to stand almost free, loosely linked with smaller shrubs or herbaceous groups. Smaller plants, such as those listed on p. 31, can flow round and between the groups like water round rocks.

Except in an alpine garden, a single small herbaceous plant makes no impact; larger bushy plants like the herbaceous peony can, however, be planted singly. Upright plants like phlox look better in groups of three or more; so do irises, which also serve to prop up taller plants, making ugly staking unnecessary. A list of herbaceous perennials that need little or no support is given on p. 32.

Plants less than two feet tall, like geums and columbines, are

# Town Gardens to Live In

Fig. 7. *Plan of a garden in Rye. The lines of the garden direct the eye towards the marsh landscape. The accompanying photographs illustrate the different stages*

6. *The garden in Rye after laying the paving, but before planting*

7. *After the larger plants had been put in*

8. *The completed garden*

more effective in groups of five or more (not rows). A few plants – the large mullein (*Verbascum bombyciferum*, syn. *V.* Broussa), acanthus and *Ligularia dentata* – can be treated like sculpture, to be seen in isolation either in the planting bed or growing out of paving, while the graceful feathery fennel (*Foeniculum vulgare* or *F. v.* Purpureum) is a good substitute for a fountain. Plants that flower early in the summer, poppies for instance, should be placed where their dying leaves will be partly hidden by the developing foliage of other plants like catmint or lavender.

There are no hard and fast rules about how much space to leave between plants. With shrubs, it depends on how long you are prepared to wait until the plants join up, and whether the growing conditions (soil, aspect, etc.) are favourable. If you are in a hurry, you might allow about three-quarters of the plant's span, or width, as given in the nursery catalogues. A very rough guide to economical planting of groups of the same species is as follows: large shrubs, 4 ft apart; medium shrubs, 3 ft; small shrubs and large herbaceous plants, 2 ft; medium herbaceous plants, $1\frac{1}{2}$ ft; small herbaceous plants, 1 ft. Small or medium plants near the front of a bed should ideally be near enough to the edge to cover the earth but not spread beyond the bed, unless it is edged with stone, as in pl. 85.

Colour arrangements depend on individual taste, though there is one combination which should be avoided. Reds with a lot of yellow in them clash harshly with reds that have a blue base, as anyone who has tried mixing Super Star roses with crimson ones will know. Colour distributed evenly over the garden may be spread too thin and look spotty. Small colonies of plants of differing heights that flower at roughly the same time make a stronger impression; when not in bloom, their leaves make a green foil for neighbouring groups with a different flowering period. Colours within a group may be in startling contrast with one another; or they may blend different shades in the same colour range – a group of pale yellow *Achillea* Moonshine, creamy-white floribunda roses and apricot day lilies would be an example.

Shrubs on their own need less attention than a mixed bed. Evergreens are a godsend in winter, and are more likely to do well in a town garden now that the Clean Air Act has reduced pollution. But the unrelieved gloom of evergreens has a limited appeal; they need

## The Bones of Design

to be mixed with bush roses or shrubs of contrasting foliage to bring in splashes of light. Grey, red or variegated foliage gives contrast of colour; a few examples of each are listed on p. 32. Contrast of form will also add interest: for example, a feathery bamboo (*Arundinaria murieliae* or *A. nitida*) may be combined with the spiky *Mahonia bealei* and dark, shiny-leaved camellias, rhododendrons or *Skimmia japonica* Foremanii.

Whatever the basic planting, extra colour can be added by double use of ground. Creamy-pink *Tulipa kaufmanniana* planted in front of peonies will flower when the red spears of the peonies are only just pushing their way through the earth. Later, when the tulips die down, they will be protected from excessive heat by the expanding leaves of the peony. Snowdrops round the foot of a bush rose will have flowered before the bush begins to spread with the weight of leaves and flowers. Lilies can come through light ground cover or small shrubs.

Another form of double use is to leave pockets between shrubs or large herbaceous plants and fill them with spring bulbs followed by annuals or bedding plants such as petunias or dahlias (not pelargoniums, most of them are too stiff in habit). Finally, there are those stand-bys of most town gardeners, bulbs and annuals in pots (see pp. 152-3).

Planting design is a complex subject about which it is impossible to lay down hard and fast rules that will guarantee success. Perhaps the best advice is to do as Gertrude Jekyll did and base your designs on observation of how plants grow in their natural habitat.

*Some ground-cover plants*

Herbaceous perennials: *Bergenia cordifolia* and *B.* Silver Light, *Campanula poscharskyana, Doronicum cordifolia, Geranium* Russell Prichard and *G. macrorrhizum, Heuchera tiarelloides* Bridget Bloom, London pride (*Saxifraga umbrosa*), dwarf evening primrose (*Oenothera missouriensis*), *Tiarella cordifolia* (foam flower).

Shrubby: *Cornus canadensis, Cotoneaster dammeri* (spreads quickly) and *C. congestus, Erica carnea, Euonymus fortunei* Silver Queen, hebes (several), *Iberis sempervirens* Snowflake, ivies (*Hedera helix* and *H. colchica* and others), *Pachysandra terminalis*, rhododendron (dwarf varieties).

Town Gardens to Live In

*Herbaceous perennials needing little support*

Acanthus, Aconitum (monk's hood), anemones (Japanese), *Artemisia ludoviciana* (white sage), *Aruncus dioicus* (goat's beard), astilbes (several), *Campanula lactiflora* and *C. latifolia*, *Chrysanthemum maximum*, *Clematis integrifolia*, *Crambe cordifolia*, day lilies (*Hemerocallis*) – some, *Echinacea purpurea*, *Euphorbia characias* and *E. wulfenii*, *Echinops* (globe thistle), foxgloves (*Digitalis purpurea*), *Gypsophila* Bristol Fairy and Flamingo, heleniums (several), iris (bearded), kniphofias, ligularias (several), *Lysimachia punctata* (loose-strife), *Monarda* (bergamot), peonies (some), phlox (several), poppies (oriental), *Romneya coulteri* (tree poppy), thalictrums (some).

*Some shrubs to contrast with evergreens*

Grey: *Buddleia alternifolia* and *B. fallowiana*, *Elaeagnus angustifolia*, *E. commutata* and *E. macrophylla*, *Hebe glaucophylla*, *Hippophaë rhamnoides* (sea buckthorn), lavender, *Olearia mollis*, potentillas (several), *Santolina chamaecyparissus*, *Senecio greyi* or *S. laxifolius*.

Red: *Acer palmatum* Atropurpureum and *A. p.* Dissectum Atropurpureum (Japanese maples), azaleas (mollis varieties), *Berberis thunbergii* Atropurpurea, *Cotinus coggygria* Royal Purple or *C.* Rubrifolius (purple smoke bush), *Prunus cistena*.

Variegated: *Cornus alba* Elegantissima, *Cotoneaster horizontalis* Variegatus, *Daphne odora* Aureomarginata, *Elaeagnus pungens* Maculata, *Euonymus fortunei* (several), hebes (several), ivies (*Hedera colchica* Variegata and *H. helix* Aureovariegata), *Philadelphus coronarius* Variegatus, *Phormium tenax* Variegatum (New Zealand flax).

*Annuals and bedding for planting pockets*

*Alyssum maritimum* (sweet alyssum), antirrhinum, begonia (fibrous-rooted), calendula (pot marigold, from seed), dahlia (small), *Echium* Blue Bedder (from seed), eschscholzia (from seed), nicotiana, petunia, *Phlox drummondii*, polyanthus, viola, wallflower, zinnia.

## 2  Six Gardens

It is virtually impossible for anyone to design a garden without borrowing ideas from gardens they have seen and experienced. These may range from a layman's garden to one designed by a highly skilled professional; both have a contribution to make. The six examples that follow are the work of professional designers and have been included in this do-it-yourself book on garden design because, highly sophisticated though they are, studying them may suggest ideas that could be translated into your own garden in a simpler form. Between them they demonstrate nearly all the basic principles of town garden design.

### A SMALL LONDON GARDEN, *designed by John Brookes*

The garden opens up from an area outside a semi-basement in a series of steps that end in a small sitting space with barbecue. A spiral stair leads to a roof garden.

9.

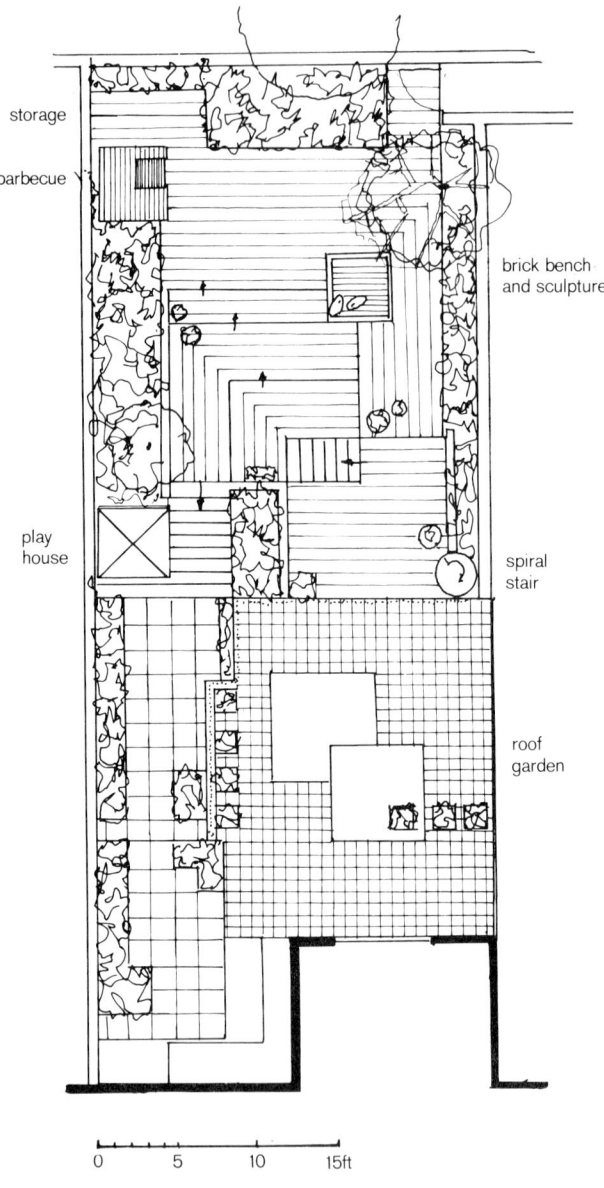

Fig. 8. *A small London garden*

## Six Gardens

This is an example of the creative use of waste. The soil dug out in widening the area at the bottom has been used to build up the ground above, enabling the designer to manipulate the different levels (and saving money in the process – carting away soil is expensive). The use of a single hard material throughout avoids fragmentation of the small plot, and skilful modelling gives an extra dimension. This low-maintenance garden provides plenty of casual sitting space but little room for plants, but the terraces, if unpaved, could be used for planting (see p. 17 for a note on soil).

## *A TOWN GARDEN IN WEST GERMANY,*
*designed by Hans Luz*

Designed on a small plot and surrounded by high walls to give privacy, the garden at ground level is mostly in shadow. Space for sitting and for growing plants had therefore to be created elsewhere. The main outdoor sitting space (pl. 127) is on the flat roof of a one-storey block linked to the two-storey house. It is reached through a series of terraces luxuriant with foliage. On a smaller scale, a similar leafy approach could be achieved by a raised bed with a small upright tree and some self-clinging climbers, backed up by pots on strong wooden staging and ledges (pl. 133) or in metal wall-brackets (pl. 136).

10.

# Town Gardens to Live In

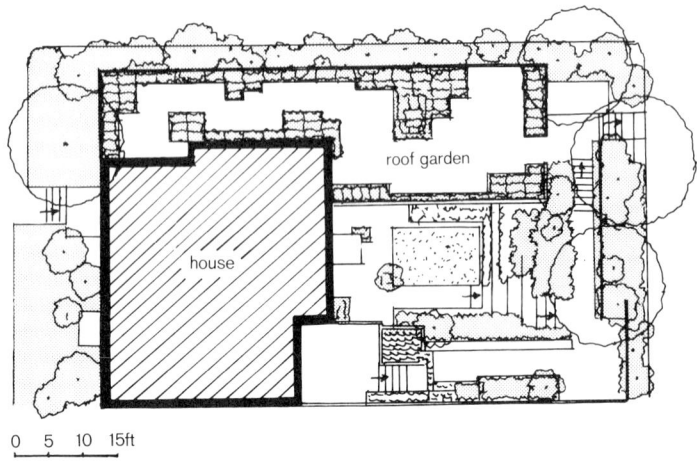

Fig. 9. *A town garden in West Germany*

Six Gardens

*A SMALL SUBURBAN GARDEN, designed by John Brookes*

The width of the garden (about thirty feet) is greater than its length (about twenty feet); by drawing attention to the width, the garden is made to seem quite large. From a paved, pergola-enclosed sitting space near the house, the design swings away diagonally to the right, ending in dense foliage. Two shallow changes of level increase the sense of movement in what would otherwise be a flat, static plot. The two plans illustrate the step-by-step process of planting design.

12.

# Town Gardens to Live In

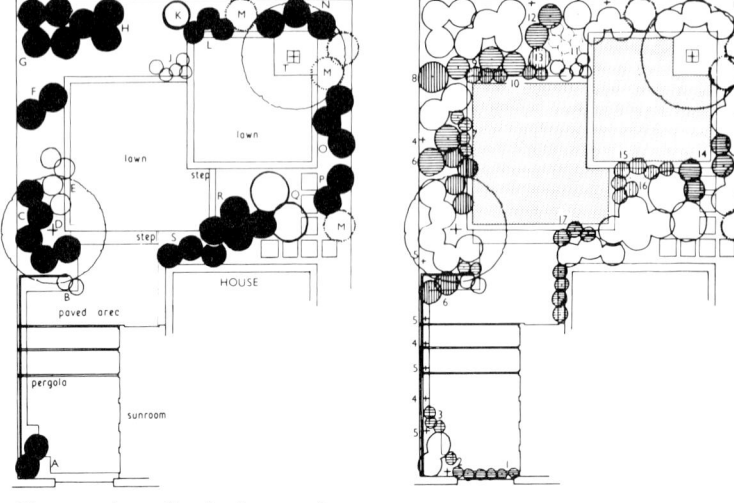

Fig. 10. *A small suburban garden*

Left: *skeleton planting of trees, evergreens and large deciduous shrubs*
Right: *subsequent infill planting of smaller deciduous shrubs and herbaceous material*

Skeleton shrubs

A  *Fatsia japonica* 2
B  *Yucca flaccida* 2
C  *Cotoneaster salicifolius* 5
D  *Prunus subhirtella* Autumnalis 1
E  *Cytisus scoparius* Sulphureus 4
F  *Camellia (white)* 2
G  *Pyracantha atalantioides* 3
H  *Escallonia* Donard Star 4
J  *Kniphofia caulescens* 5
K  *Cotinus coggygria* Foliis Purpureis 1
L  *Rosmarinus* Pyramidalis 3
M  *Ceanothus burkwoodii* 3
N  *Chamaecyparis wissellii* 4
O  *Viburnum tinus* 3
P  *Genista aetnensis* 2
Q  *Rhus typhina* Laciniata 2
R  *Choisya ternata* 4
S  *Mahonia bealei* 3
T  *Ficus carica* 1

Infill planting

1  *Bergenia cordifolia* 7
2  *Existing wisteria*
3  *Dryopteris filix-mas* 3
4  *Hedera canariensis*
5  *Clematis montana*
6  *Choisya ternata* 2
7  *Anaphalis triplinervis* 4
8  *Forsythia suspensa atrocaulis* 1
9  *Shrub roses* 3
10  *Salvia officinalis purpurescens* 5
11  *Floribunda roses* 8
12  *Buddleia davidii* 2
13  *Paeonia lutea ludlowii* 1
14  *Hydrangea paniculata* Grandiflora 4
15  *Lavendula spica* Hidcote 7
16  *Agapanthus* Headbourne Hybrids 3
17  *Senecio laxifolius* 7
18  *Climbing rose*

13. *Looking back at the enclosed sitting space in the small suburban garden*

## *A LARGE SUBURBAN GARDEN*, designed by John Brookes

An example of the country brought to town. The house stands on a slope overlooking Hampstead Heath, with the ground rising sharply behind it to a terrace laid out as a herb garden (pl. 120). In winter, the first-floor living rooms and balcony have superb views of Highgate Ponds. In summer, the flowing lines of the garden melt into the trees, consciously echoing the contours and woodlands of the Heath (pl. 14). Existing trees have been worked into the design, to great effect. Low retaining walls enclose a group between the drive and the lawn (pl. 15), making a barrier that snakes downhill towards the entrance gate. The ground cover is chosen for a shady situation: rose of Sharon (*Hypericum calycinum*), woodruff (*Asperula odorata*), variegated ivy (*Hedera colchica* Variegata) and occasional low shrubs. Near the gate a three-stemmed arbutus emerges like sculpture from a froth of *Lonicera pileata* (pl. 16). The steep bank

14.

behind the house, in shade for much of the day, is planted with groups of variegated dogwood (*Cornus alba* Elegantissima) and ground cover of *Cotoneaster dammeri*. An easily maintained garden, except for the herb garden.

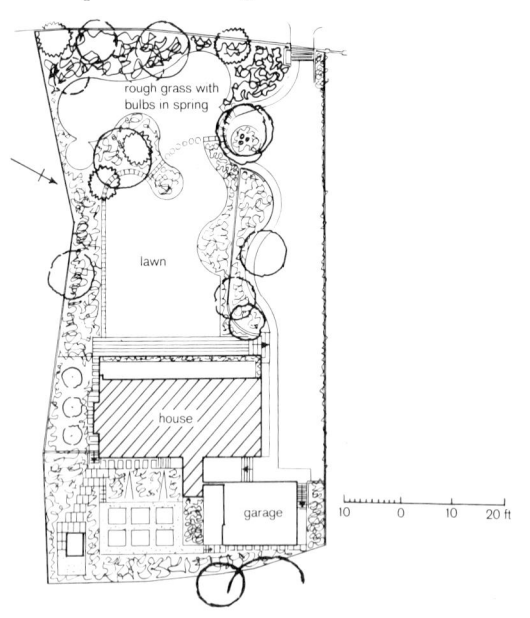

Fig. 11. *A large suburban garden*

15.

16.

17.

Town Gardens to Live In

## A SMALL GARDEN IN A COUNTRY TOWN,
*designed by A. du Gard Pasley*

How to make a plus out of a minus: the rubble originally covering the plot was collected into the awkwardly pointed, almost unusable top-left-hand corner to make a base for stone steps and a terrace with sculpture. With the addition of a small pool, this became the focal point of the garden, visible from the main rooms of the house. Unfortunately, a fine *Cotoneaster frigida* shown on the plan had later to be cut down and the line of the paving altered.

18.

Six Gardens

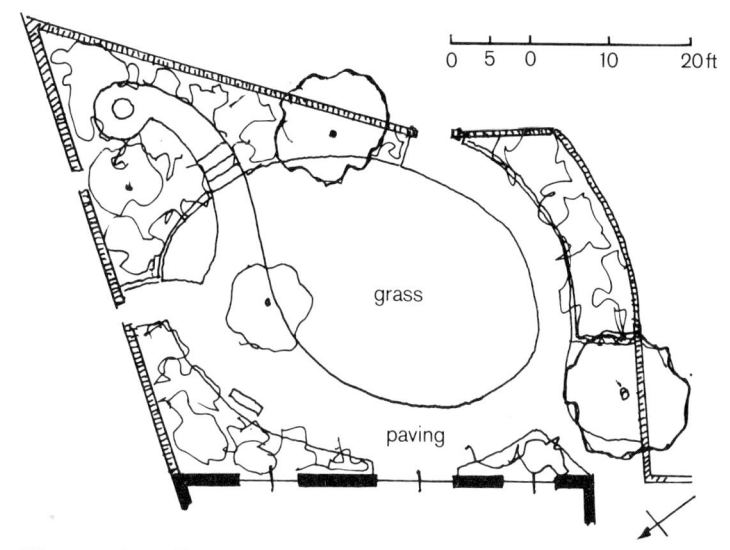

Fig. 12. *A small garden in a country town*

The swing of the curves breaks up the rectangular shape of the site in a design which is reminiscent of the Victorian villa garden of the mid nineteenth century.

## A HOUSING-ESTATE GARDEN,
*designed by the Town Development Division of the Greater London Council (job architect: John Talbot)*

Mass production and the individual confront each other in a housing-estate garden and must somehow come to terms. Some privacy from neighbours is the first need, achieved here by wattle hurdles on one side and a brick wall on the other. A party wall only $4\frac{1}{2}$ in. thick is possible if it is broken up into bays, and these make attractive recesses for climbing plants on both sides of the wall. The paving slabs are arranged to give access to the end of the garden. There is no grass.

Planting along the right-hand side of the picture (pl. 19) is chiefly ground cover like *Bergenia* Silver Light and rose of Sharon (*Hypericum calycinum*), with a few large shrubs – *Amelanchier*

43

19.

20.

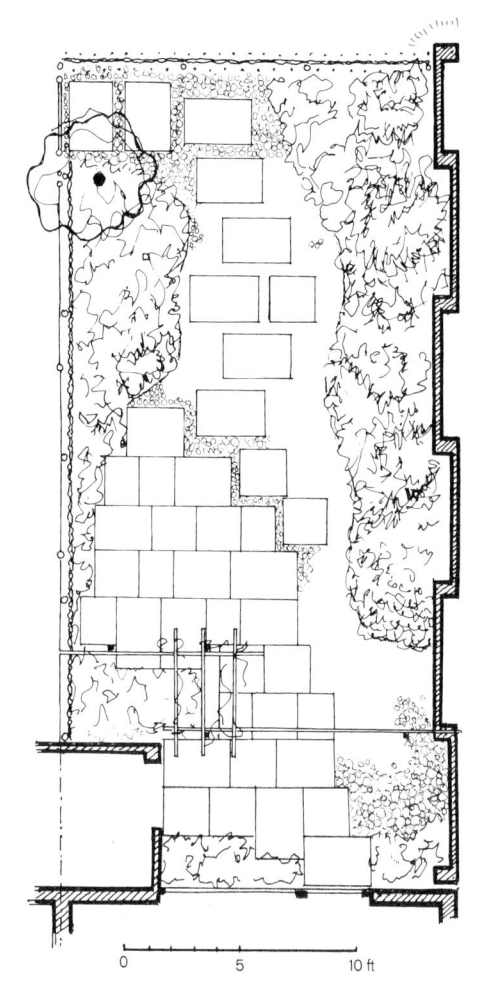

Fig. 13. *A housing-estate garden*

*canadensis* and a witch hazel (*Hamamelis mollis*) – and a plot for rhubarb and marrows at the far end. On the left is a herb bed with runner beans against the wall; beyond it, a group of evergreen shrubs breaks up the rectangular space.

## 3  Creating an Illusion

Most gardeners indulge in some form of make-believe. Some may just want to make their garden look larger than it is, but for many the motives are more deeply rooted: to shut out not only their immediate physical surroundings but the world at large, and by deceiving the eye, to give the imagination freedom to roam.

In planning garden illusions the three most important points to remember are:

1. There must be no feeling of being confined within a geometrical shape;
2. A green silhouette should be created, to blot out or break up the silhouette of surrounding buildings;
3. The whole of the garden should not be seen at a glance; this creates a sense of mystery.

21. *An Islington garden in 1958*

## Creating an Illusion

There are useful devices that help to make the garden seem larger than it is:

1. Emphasis on the longest dimension.
2. Use of false perspective.
3. Use of planting to create a sense of distance (pp. 51–2).

A garden in Islington, London (fig. 14), illustrates the effectiveness of two of these devices for increasing the apparent size of a garden: the first photograph (pl. 21), showing the garden as an empty, brick-enclosed rectangle, was taken in 1958; the second (pl. 22) was taken some fifteen years later.

1. The longest dimension in any garden is the distance between two opposite corners, i.e. from bottom left to top right or the other way about. Anything that can be done to emphasize this line will have the effect of making the garden seem longer than it really is. In the Islington garden, the eye is invited to travel along just such a diagonal. Visually, the garden veers slightly from left to right, crossing from the house door in the bottom left-hand corner of the plan towards the paved sitting space on the right, and passing it to

22. *The same garden in 1973*

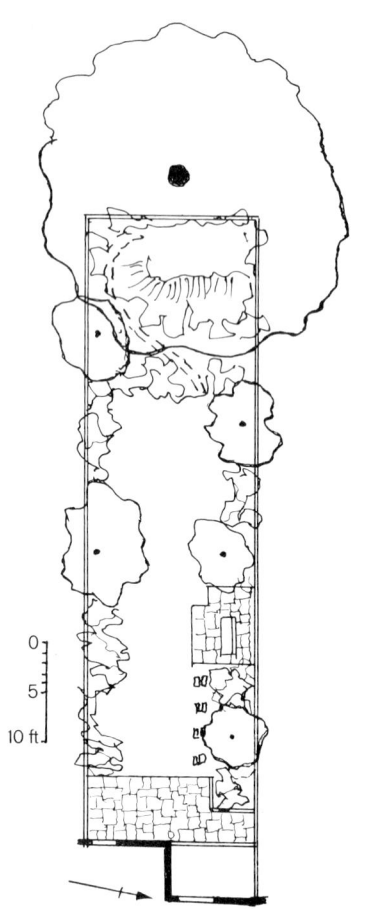

Fig. 14. *A garden in Islington*

*Planting: left side* – *bay tree* (Laurus nobilis), Fuchsia magellanica *Versicolor, Lilac* (Syringa vulgaris *Souvenir de Louis Späth*), Sarcococca humilis, *small periwinkle* (Vinca minor, *bearded iris,* Hydrangea petiolaris, *London pride* (Saxifraga umbrosa), Campanula poscharskyana; *back* – Magnolia × soulangeana, Fatsia japonica, Mahonia bealei, Euphorbia wulfenii, Rhododendron *Bluebird,* Epimedium × versicolor *Sulphureum*; *right side* – Rosa *Nevada, hybrid musk rose Felicia, climbing roses Sympathie and Étoile de Hollande,* Clematis *Lasurstern, Lavender* (Lavandula spica *Munstead*), Potentilla arbuscula *Beesii,* Iris *Austrian Blue and Greenspot,* Campanula poscharskyana *and floribunda roses*

## Creating an Illusion

become lost in the green caverns of the planting at the end of the garden. The right-hand side of the garden is given over to roses and a few herbaceous plants.

Had the house door been on the right, a different arrangement would have been needed, possibly with the sitting-space nearest the house and the rose-bed beyond, facing a curve of shade-tolerant plants on the left which narrowed towards the far end.

2. To create the impression that a garden continues beyond what is seen at first glance, it is worth sacrificing space at the far end in order to introduce, some ten feet from the rear boundary, a trellis, hedge or other not completely impenetrable barrier, arranged so as to hint at unseen excitements beyond, although in fact the compost heap and potting shed are all that lurk in the shadows. In the Islington garden, which ends in a fairly steep bank overhung by a chestnut tree in the next garden, the same effect has been achieved by bringing forward a belt of shrub planting that is deep enough to give room for a winding upward path that looks romantic and inviting although its only purpose is a practical one.

The garden owes its sense of mystery and seclusion to the profusion of the plants. This is largely due to the owner's acceptance of the conditions for growth, choosing only plants which have a good chance of succeeding. Since many town gardens have poor soil and a good deal of shade, the plant list is given on p. 48.

A south London garden designed and made by the owner only two years ago mixes ideas from two sources – the traditional Japanese garden and the small French formal garden. The plan (fig. 15) shows the main part of the garden to be almost a square, divided into two by a winding central grass path between low box hedges, with a mowing strip of cobbles set below the level of the turf. Seen from inside the house (pl. 23), the path swings to the left, narrowing as it goes until the point at which it bends back to the right; at the bend, it is only half as wide as at the start. This device of falsifying the perspective has the effect of making the path look longer than it really is. It can equally well be applied to a straight path.

Paths that curve for no particular reason can sometimes look silly. The line of this path has been carefully worked out to do

23. *The view from the house*

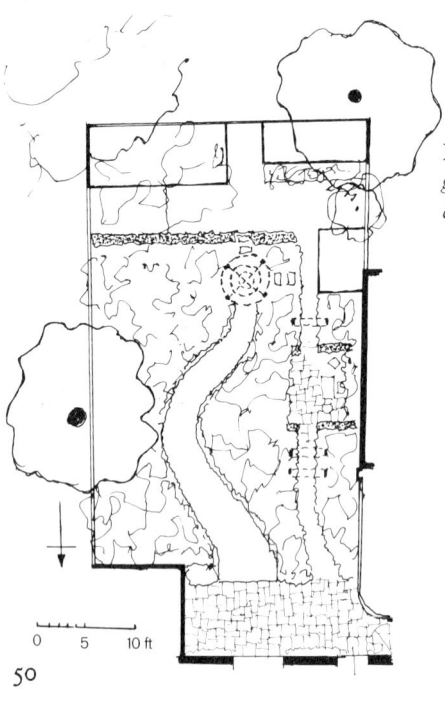

Fig. 15. *A south London garden based on Japanese and French traditions*

50

*24. Looking back at the house*

several things. First, by pointing towards the left side of the garden it draws attention to a fine tree of heaven (*Ailanthus altissima*) in the next garden, so that one forgets to look to the right, where a blank concrete wall overlooks the garden. The lesson here is that if you can't hide an ugly object, you can try to distract attention from it. If there had been no object of interest already to hand, one could easily have been created by planting a striking tree such as a golden acacia (*Robinia pseudoacacia* Frisia) or silver-leaved pear (*Pyrus salicifolia* Pendula).

Having achieved its purpose of drawing attention to the left side of the garden, the path then turns back towards the wrought iron feature in the centre and joins up with the paths to the other parts of the garden. The resulting curves create two irregular spaces, each of which is deep enough in places to accommodate quite large shrubs.

Planting plays a major part in the creation of an illusion. The sides of this garden disappear in the dark recesses of camellias, rhododendrons and other evergreens, and these in turn merge with the trees in the adjoining gardens. By contrast, the detail near the

## Town Gardens to Live In

house is small, sharply defined and full of interest. The whole garden has been thought of in terms of foreground, middle distance and the 'borrowed landscape' (to use a Japanese term) of the neighbours' trees. But although the design has been worked out much as an artist arranges the composition of a landscape painting, this is a picture into which one can walk.

A favourite Japanese device for creating a sense of distance also uses a form of false perspective. By placing one or two isolated medium-sized plants (3–4 ft) near the front of a bed and a few smaller ones (2–2½ ft) further back, with a gap of about 4 ft between, the distance between the two groups will be made to look greater than it is in reality. It is dangerous to give examples, because the height to which a plant will grow depends on local circumstances, but two tentative suggestions will convey the rough idea: (*a*) a few spikes of mullein (*Verbascum* Gainsborough or the taller *V. vernale*) near the front, mounds of purple sage (*Salvia officinalis* Purpurascens) at the back, with blue pools of *Campanula poscharskyana* between; or (*b*) *Potentilla fruticosa* Abbotswood near the front, *Rhododendron williamsianum* near the back, with ground cover of *Geranium macrorrhizum* or *Hebe pinguifolia* Pagei between. Lilies planted near the front are particularly useful for this kind of arrangement.

Planting can also be used to direct the eye. In the garden just described, clumps of silver-leaved plants, irregularly in line, carry the eye towards the white central feature and on still further to a sculptured plaque on the end wall in the working area, which is screened from the main garden by a beech hedge. Although colour can be used to give a sense of distance (reds stand out and seem near, blues recede), the flowers used here are mostly white; strong colour is only used in the Japanese manner, in small quantities at one time. A final Japanese touch is the tiny bamboo grove, a rustling background to conversation in the paved sitting-arbour on the right of the plan.

*25. Garden of a north London terrace house*

## TERRACED HOUSING

This presents gardeners with a slightly different set of problems. On the one hand, since terraces often back on to each other, the space between acts as a lung, often big enough for a few large trees. These combine with tall shrubs to give privacy and need not make flower-growing impossible, although they do narrow the choice. On the other, the gardens are often long and narrow, a difficult shape to handle. The best way to handle long, thin gardens is to break them up into two or three separate compartments of varying lengths. The north London garden in pl. 25, which is 120 feet long, makes its first division with a paved sitting area set among roses and shrubs. A second, less flowery, compartment ends in a shaded sitting space; beyond this is the working area for compost and storage. The width between the walls is only fifteen feet, yet within this narrow space a sense of well-proportioned seclusion has been created.

Town Gardens to Live In

The separation of compartments in this garden is very gentle. A sharper division, using a hedge or trellis, gives a greater sense of moving from one space to another and also makes it possible to frame a view in the opening between the two spaces. A framed view is always more powerful than an unframed one; by concentrating and limiting the view, it heightens anticipation. Pl. 26 shows a nostalgic evocation of a cottage garden. Other possible view-framers could be: elegant wrought-iron arches as in pl. 23, perhaps smothered with jasmine or honeysuckle; yew, whose dark forms add to the brightness of the flowers beyond; laburnum or apples trained into an arch. The jasmine will need frequent pruning.

Another way of confusing the boundaries, used in a garden at Golders Green (pl. 27), is only suitable for a square or broad garden, where there is plenty of width to play with. The planting along the perimeter is brought forward at intervals in two or three thrusting curves, each projecting further than the previous one, to give a suggestion of glades. In essence, this is a variation on the Islington garden (fig. 14, pls. 21 and 22), adapted to suit the needs of the site, and underlies the need to look carefully at your plot.

26. *A framed view in a St John's Wood garden*

27. *The boundary treatment in a Golders Green garden*

## 4 *The Garden Floor*

In very small gardens, much depends on the pattern, material and texture of the hard surfaces and their relationship to the more complex texture of the green areas. Unfortunately, daydreams of velvet lawns can seldom be realized in tightly enclosed small spaces. Too much wear and too little light and air will soon reduce a small grass plot to a sad patch of earth with a few green wisps. There are also problems of maintaining and storing a lawn-mower in an area where every inch is precious. On the other hand, too large an expanse of paving is hard on the eye as well as the feet. Its effect can be softened by blocks of planting or even by planting between the joints of the paving.

A simple pattern of paving and planting, using plots of ivy in place of grass, can be restful, effective and easy to maintain. Ivy round the base of a tree or large shrub has a certain elegance if it is

28. *Garden in St John's Wood* (see fig. 16)

## Town Gardens to Live In

kept trim and shining clean. Low evergreens that also lend themselves to this rather geometrical block treatment are *Sarcococca humilis*, dwarf box, *Pachysandra terminalis* and *Lonicera pileata*. Keeping the planting at a low level helps to make the most of a small space. It also puts more emphasis on the boundaries, which should be at least partly green clad so as to offset the paved floor, and needs at least one small tree or large shrub to break up the flatness. This type of garden is ideal for owners with little spare time. Those who have time, and enjoy gardening, can fill the planting spaces with their favourite shrubs and flowers. The result is softer and richer, even slightly mysterious if part of the garden is hidden by tall shrubs.

Small plants in cracks between paving stones are another way of breaking up an expanse of paving; you also gain extra growing space. Pls. 41–3 show different arrangements. Alpine plants can be used in this way. But in gardens with full sun all day long, hard paving can become so hot as to affect the plants, both by drying up the soil and by reflected heat; Mediterranean-type plants, such as cistus, lavender and helianthemum, which are more used to dry heat, will do better in such conditions. Brick paving also helps; if it is well hosed down, it quickly soaks up the water and passes it to the plants.

Gardens that are too small for planting beds must rely on the softening effect of groups of plants in pots; these can include shrubs as well as colourful bedding plants, annuals and bulbs (see chapter 14).

In working out a design, make sure that one of your two ingredients – paving and green areas – dominates over the other. As a very rough guide, one-third of one and two-thirds of the other is more satisfying than half and half. The way the garden is to be used will decide which way round it is to be: party-givers need more hard surfaces than plant-lovers. The pattern that emerges will then be governed by the choice of paving material. This in turn will be related to the size of the garden and, to a lesser extent, the material of which the house is built. If, for example, your house is of brick, a small amount of brick in the ground pattern will help to weld garden and house together.

The Garden Floor

29. Single plants between cracks in stone paving

30. An irregular pattern of natural stones and small plants

31. The geometry of precast concrete paving softened by plants like mind your own business (Helxine soleirolii)

Town Gardens to Live In

## BRICK

Brick has many points in its favour. Being a small unit, it is one of the easiest means of making a curved path or making slight changes of level. It can be laid in various ways: in patterns such as herringbone or basket-weave (pl. 32); lengthways in a path to indicate direction; crossways to make a path seem wider (pl. 33). New

*32. Brick basket-weave paving*

*33. Bricks laid crossways on a path to make it look wider*

34. *Setts and concrete paving in a garden at Warwick*

35. *Brick and concrete paving at Stevenage*

bricks are expensive. So is the cost of labour if you can't lay them yourself, but they can be laid by a skilled amateur. Some brick manufacturers sell substandard bricks at the brickfield at a lower price. Second-hand bricks which are cheaper can sometimes be picked up from a builders' merchant. Ask them which is the best brick for the purpose. Wire-cut bricks have a slightly textured surface, which prevents slipperiness when wet, and are frost-resistant. A saving of up to 50 per cent can be made by using bricks which do not have a hollow (called a frog) on both their broad faces, and laying them with the $9 \times 4\frac{1}{2}$ in. face uppermost, rather than their $9 \times 3$ in. side. Bricks can be laid on 3–4 in. of hardcore topped by a 1-in. layer of sharp builder's sand. The joints can either be mortared (see p. 165) or filled with more sharp sand, well watered in. If you want to encourage moss in the joints, top up the joints with a little bonemeal mixed with more sand.

A more economic solution is to combine brick with some other material, such as concrete, using the bricks to make a patterned framework within which the concrete slabs are contained. Two different examples of this are shown in pls. 34 and 35. In one, the concrete square is surrounded by setts; in the other, the bricks are little more than ribbons between the concrete, making a strongly patterned setting for the foliage of trees and the activities of human beings. Setts (generally cut into cubes or rectangles) are expensive. You could get a similar effect to pl. 34 with bricks. Setts are useful for paving round tree roots (pl. 36).

36. *Granite setts being laid round the roots of a tree. The joints were later filled with soil*

37. *A pattern of granite setts with grass joints*

## CONCRETE

Precast concrete slabs are now made commercially in various sizes and colours. Beware of highly-coloured ones if you want a garden you can relax in. Many are textured to simulate natural stone: Pennine stone from Marshall's of Halifax; Marley Landscape Paving (instructions for laying are given on p. 169). If you want something different, the Cement and Concrete Association publish two excellent free booklets (see p. 184) with detailed explanations and drawings to show how to make your own. An interesting texture can be produced by laying cobbles in wet concrete (pl. 39), but flattish cobbles must be used if the area is to be walked on. This is a skilled operation but not beyond the powers of the experienced, and it is described on p. 172. Concrete slabs combine well with lime

38. *Home-made concrete slabs in two tones on which concentric circles have been marked out while the concrete was still soft. Only the light-toned slabs are marked. The dark slabs were made first, providing a base to stand on while the marking was done*

*39. Cobbles and concrete at Wexham Springs*

*40. Uni-Block paving and loose gravel*

chippings, in much the same way as the York stone and gravel floor pattern shown in fig. 16.

Recently, a new type of paving material has been introduced: Monolok stones, made by Mono Concrete, and Uni-Block, by British Dredging Aggregates Ltd (pl. 40). The texture is not unlike carpets in a house; small areas of it would be very suitable in an outdoor room.

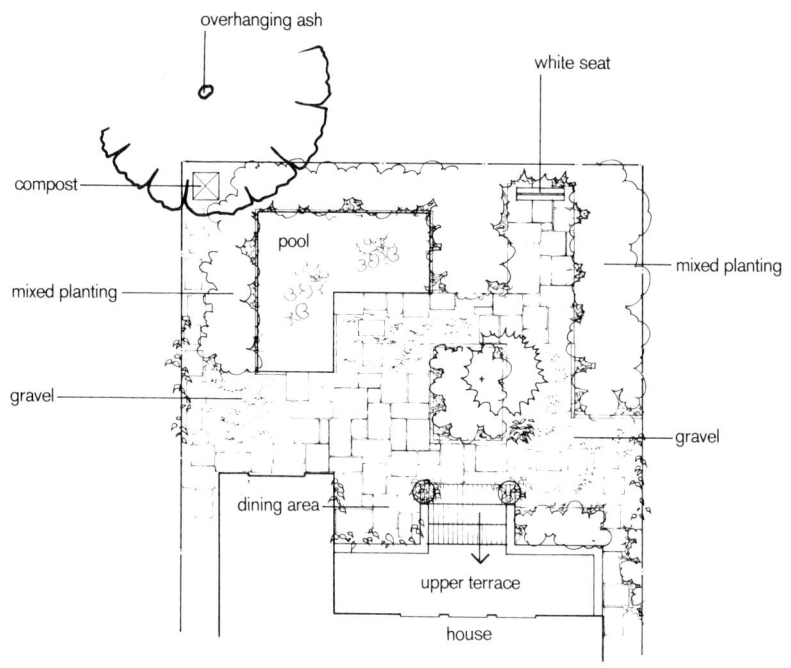

Fig. 16. *Plan of the garden in north-west London (pl. 28) in which the planting plays a lesser role than the paving. The hard surface is a combination of York stone and gravel*

## STONE

Stone is very much more expensive than brick or concrete, but old pavings are still available at times from local councils and are attractively weathered, whereas new York stone is severe in tone. Rectangular paving is more harmonious than the somewhat restless crazy paving. It can be laid on a 1-in. layer of sand or on a 3-in. bed of hardcore with a touch of mortar on the underside of each corner. Joints can be left open for planting or filled with mortar. The stones can also be simply butt-joined, in which case the whole area to be paved should first be treated with weed-killer.

If York stone is available, it is cheaper to eke it out with gravel, as in pl. 28. Gravel should have a well-compacted 4-in. base of hardcore laid on earth which has been treated with a non-selective weedkiller. The gravel should also be well rolled; loose gravel is

63

41. *Stone and granite setts in a Danish garden*

uncomfortable to walk on. The final thickness of the gravel layer should be about two inches. Planting beds and gravel areas should be separated by narrow surrounds of stone, timber or brick on edge, to prevent gravel spreading on to the beds.

All hard surfaces should be laid with a slight but imperceptible slope in one direction, to allow surplus rainwater to run off: brick and concrete approximately 2 in. in 10 ft; stone or concrete paving slabs, 1 in. in 6 ft; gravel, 1 in. in 10 ft.

To help you to compare costs, here are the approximate 1977 prices, per square yard, of various paving materials supplied and laid on hardcore, where necessary, by outside labour: gravel, £1.60; pre-cast concrete slabs, £3.20 (more for proprietary brands); brick, £12.00; granite setts, new, £14.00; granite setts, second-hand, £13.00; York stone, new, £21.20; York stone, second-hand, £11.30. This does not include excavation, soil stripping or VAT.

## TIMBER

Timber decking is an attractive material, but only suitable for small sheltered areas, owing to its slipperiness when wet. It is useful when a change of floor material seems called for. The thick slats, about 4-in. wide, with $\frac{1}{8}$-in. gaps between to allow rainwater to run away, are laid on joists and treated with preservative.

# The Garden Floor

## *GRASS*

If you decide to have a grass plot, and are going to mow it with a hand-mower, the ground should be an inch higher than the surrounding paving. One wheel of the mower can then rest on a solid base when cutting the outer edges. Where grass and planted areas meet, lay a row of mowing stones slightly below the level of the turf. (With an electric mower this is not necessary.) Newly seeded areas are best contained within a narrow timber framework (curved or straight) or a turf edging to keep the soil from spilling over until the roots of the grass consolidate the earth. Turfing, the quickest method of achieving a mature-looking lawn, costs about four times as much as seeding. This may be justified if the area involved is very small or if the grass is to be subjected to immediate hard wear – by children, for instance. Seeding involves more work and takes time to become established, but has one other advantage besides its lower cost. From the wide range of seeds stocked by most garden centres you can choose that which meets your special needs: Sutton's Green Shadow for shady gardens, Johnson's General Purpose for semi-shade and play areas, Sutton's Summer Play for hard wear. Both firms offer slow-growing mixes that need less frequent cutting. In most cases the seeds have been treated with bird-repellent. Careful levelling and preparation of the ground to get a fine stone-free tilth, followed by raking in a pre-seeding fertilizer, are important preliminaries. Directions for sowing are given on most seed packets.

Turfing may be carried out at almost any season. Spring and late summer are traditionally the best for seeding, but periods of alternating rain and sunshine at any time during the summer are equally favourable.

Town Gardens to Live In

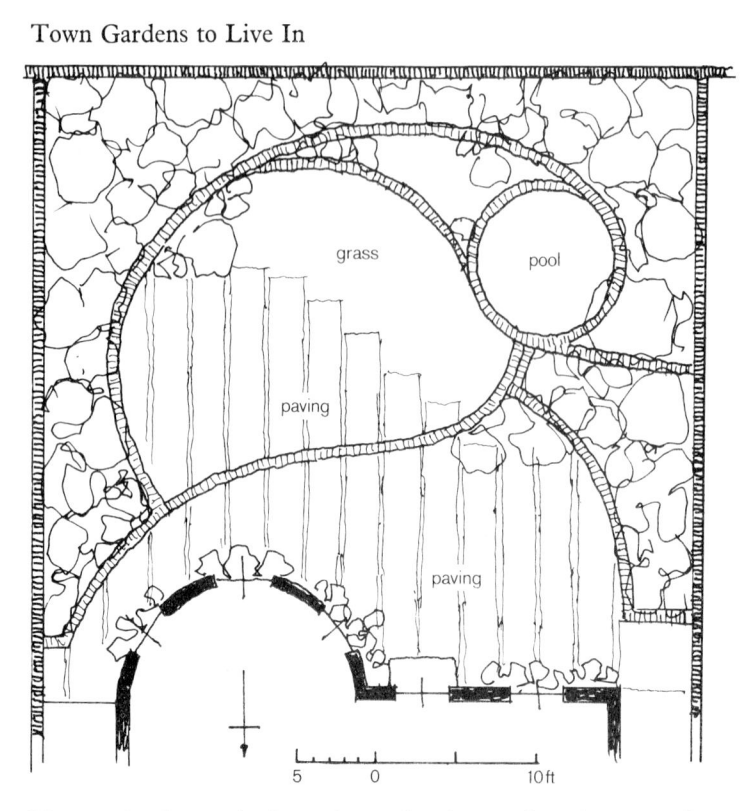

Fig. 17. *Another garden in north-west London, much used as an outdoor room for entertaining. The main ground surface is stepped to overcome the natural slope of the site and to give added interest. It is covered in pale cream binding gravel and bands of paving extending from the house. The strong semicircle of the bay window of the house inspired the circular pool and the curving shapes that spring from it. These give a sense of diagonal movement to the design and are carried out in stock brick that matches the house*

42–3. *Two views of the north-west London garden seen in fig. 17*

## 5 Walls and Screens

Although the treatment of the enclosing wall, fence or hedge barely features on the plan, it can be decisive in establishing the character of the garden. Briefly, the question is: whether to lose or use the boundaries.

The owner of an outdoor room will probably want to make the walls a part of his design. But the enthusiast for informality will use planting to blot out the boundaries and disguise the rigidity of the space enclosed. Anyone unfortunate enough to be hemmed in by wire-mesh or chain-link fencing will try to do the same, perhaps combining planting with wattle hurdles or a wooden fence near the house, to give immediate seclusion. Hurdles are one of the cheapest means of getting immediate, solid and semi-permanent protection. They are generally six feet wide and are made in varying heights from two to six feet. They need support and should be fastened by wires to wooden posts at the sides (pl. 44). Wattle is said to last for only ten years, but it often survives much longer (pl. 45). Avoid the harsh machine-made fence of thin interwoven ribbons of wood; it begins to rot before it has had time to mature, and never blends with planting.

*44. Wattle hurdles round a housing estate garden at Milton Keynes New Town*

*45. A thirty-year old wattle screen*

## Walls and Screens

If your garden boundaries are of wire-mesh or chain-link fencing and you want to spend as little as possible on covering them, evergreen honeysuckle (*Lonicera japonica* Halliana) planted ten feet apart and trained to spread evenly will cover the fencing in about three years (see pl. 51). Russian vine (*Polygonum baldschuanicum*) is even faster and has pretty white flowers in late summer, but it is not evergreen and is an untidy grower. Climbing roses and *Clematis montana* (white or pink flowers) can be trained to hide the top part of the fence; the long new rose growths should be shortened by about a third and bent gently into a curve, with the tip tied to the top of the fence. This is a job for winter. Ivy also gives good cover.

A useful timber fence for new housing estates, where wind is more of a problem than in built-up areas, is one in which alternate uprights are fixed to the back of the cross-bars, instead of all being fixed to the front (pl. 46). This leaves gaps between the uprights, letting air filter into the garden (which is good for the plants) and dispersing strong winds evenly over the area; high winds passing over a solid barrier drop sharply on the supposedly sheltered side, creating destructive turbulence.

Hedges give the same kind of protection from wind, but they take time to become established. Beware of planting hedges of quick-growing thuja or *Cupressus macrocarpa*. Their glaucous leaves collect dirt and are not cleaned by rain, making them unsuitable for town gardens. They also tend to become woody at the base and

46. *A fence on a housing estate at Milton Keynes. Alternate uprights are fixed to the back of the cross-bars, leaving gaps through which air can pass*

*47. A fence of horizontal timbers on the same principle as pl. 46*

*48. To avoid a hard straight line at the top of the fence, the uprights vary in height*

grow too tall for the garden, and they are hungry feeders, drawing much of the goodness from the soil. Beech and privet are also rather greedy, hornbeam less so, but beech has the advantage of retaining

## Walls and Screens

its cheerful russet-coloured old leaves through the winter. The cost of hedging plants depends on their height. If you only need a short length, it is worth while paying a little more for taller plants. Beech or hornbeam 2–3 ft high cost about £1 more for ten plants than those that are 1½–2 ft. They should be planted eighteen inches apart, in staggered rows if you want a thick hedge.

Mature hedges that are boring in themselves can be brought to life by using them to support climbing roses or clematis.

Rugosa roses make a quick cheap hedge, flowering on and off for most of the summer if you choose the right varieties – Roseraie de l'Hay (purple), Alba (white), or the smaller Frau Dagmar Hastrup (pink). They take up quite a lot of room – about five feet in width – but this would not matter in a rather square garden, particularly if you wanted to make it look longer by narrowing it at the sides.

Although brick can be a beautiful material, walls that are too tall can be oppressive, so think twice before increasing the height of an existing wall in order to gain privacy. A square garden might not suffer from the change in proportions, but the effect on a long narrow garden would almost certainly be disastrous. Planting can give additional height: rampageous roses like Albéric Barbier, New Dawn, Pink Perpetué or Zéphirine Drouhin, when trained up, with their top branches bent over in a wide arc as already described, will add several inches. Or a trellis or screen against the wall at the most vulnerable point could be made a special feature, with tall planting at the sides to link it with the rest of the garden.

49. *Brick walls in a Dutch garden*

Town Gardens to Live In

Some walls are improved by a coat of pale colour-wash, bringing more light into the garden. If you are likely to have to repaint later, however, it is wise to restrict climbing plants to roses, whose stems can be detached from the wall and laid flat on the ground while the work is being done.

Ugly walls can be covered by a trellis; if made of hardwood it will last indefinitely, but the kind sold by shops and garden centres, which is cheaper, is usually of softwood and may begin to break up after six or seven years. A white-painted trellis looks crisp (pl. 50) and lasts much longer (about thirty years), but must be repainted every five years or so – a tricky operation if the trellis is thickly planted with climbers. Trellis should always be fixed to the wall with the inner vertical timbers at the back so that rain can run down and not lie on the horizontals and rot them. Another solution is to cover the wall completely with planting, which has a softening effect on the garden's acoustics. If you want quick all-over cover, evergreen honeysuckle (*Lonicera japonica* Halliana) will give it in four years (pl. 51), but it is not self-clinging and must be trained on wires. It also needs clipping from time to time. Where a wall is to be only partly covered, with thin-stemmed climbers like honeysuckle or clematis, there is a method of holding them in position

50. *Trellised walls*

51. *A north London garden whose walls are completely covered by evergreen honeysuckle* (Lonicera japonica *Halliana*) *planted ten feet apart about four years ago*

52. *The delicate tracery of* Akebia quinata *against a wall of small white tiles in a Danish garden*

Fig. 18. *Fixing a plant to a brick wall with epoxy glue*

which does less damage to the wall than a nail. Place a blob of five-minute epoxy two-part glue firmly over the centre of a 2–3 in. length of tarred twine and press it on to the surface of the wall (see fig. 18).

Solid concrete walls are less congenial to most plants than wood or brick, and there are problems of fixing, but self-clinging climbers like vines and ivies, which put out clusters of tiny tentacles, do not seem to mind and will completely cover a wall in two or three years. More interesting as a material are two wall blocks made by Mono Concrete. Honeycomb Walling Blocks (pl. 53) and Landscape Blocs (pl. 54) can be assembled in a number of ways to make a pierced wall or screen. Both are expensive, but the cost may be justified if only a short length is needed as a special feature.

53. *Honeycomb Walling Blocks*   54. *Landscape Blocs in a wall*

Walls and Screens

A less dramatic and much cheaper permanent screen can be made from ordinary roofing ridge tiles arranged in a fish-scale pattern contained within a thin stone frame (pl. 55). Other screening materials that are less expensive are bamboo (pl. 56) and timber (pl. 57). They deteriorate in the course of time (depending on the amount of exposure to the weather), but their fragile elegance fits in well with the whole idea of the garden as an outdoor room.

55. *A balustrade of roofing ridge tiles arranged in a fish-scale pattern. This technique could be adapted to make a screen*

56. *A screen of bamboos in a wooden frame*

57. *Timber screen*
58. *A wrought-iron screen and gate*

# 6 Water

Unlike plants, which need time to mature, water in any form produces instant results in a garden. Its effect may be soothing or stimulating, depending on whether it is still or animated. Nowadays, thanks to modern techniques, this is a question of individual taste or temperament rather than money – it is not expensive – and the possibilities are endless.

## POOLS

The shape may be geometrical (circle, square or rectangle), biological (in a sequence of irregular curves as in an abstract painting), or seemingly natural even when man-made. It may be stocked with plants and fish, sparkle with a fountain, make a setting for sculpture or a calm mirror for reflections.

### Reflecting pools

Water in repose can bring light into a garden by drawing down the sky (pl. 59). Its silvery gleams are especially welcome in shady

59. *A long formal pool draws light down into a narrow Kensington garden sandwiched between high buildings. To break the length, the water takes a dog-leg turn half-way along*

60. *'An entrance to the mermaid's palace' in a west London garden*

gardens, where the reflections may be of trees and mysterious shadows, 'an entrance to the mermaid's palace', to quote a seventeenth-century Chinese writer (pl. 60). But when the sun is immediately overhead, a clear sky will be reflected with a blue more intense than in pools that have no shade. Equally beautiful is the bright shimmer of reflections cast on the ceiling of a room with a pool just outside the window.

61. Hydrangea paniculata *flowerheads hang above a small brick-edged pool with miniature water lilies and* Pontederia cordata

# Water

A pool intended only for reflections need be no deeper than two to four inches, especially if the sides and bottom are painted black, so that the eye does not easily penetrate. The water should come as close as possible to the top of the surrounding paving or parapet, so as to give a sense of brimming abundance. A small pool can be filled with a hosepipe and topped up as the water evaporates. To empty it for cleaning, there should be a pipe (with a plug and some mesh over the outlet) from the bottom of the pool, leading either to the nearest land-drain or to a small soakaway – a hole in the ground, two feet in diameter and three feet deep, filled with hardcore or rubble and covered with earth, should take care of the average small pool. Larger pools are best supplied by a pipe from the house and need more drainage. A pool whose surface is raised above ground level by a low retaining wall (raised pools are safer where there are children) should have a small overflow pipe near the edge of the pool, projecting about half an inch above the level of the water (see fig. 19). Alternatively, it can be surrounded by a stone gully to take any overspill, particularly useful for fountain pools with high jets, where wind may blow spray over the edge. (Instructions for making a concrete pool are on pp. 174 ff.)

62. *A pool shaped like an ammonite, with a small fountain jet from a submersible pump. The tightly curved area is a shallow bird splash. The rest is deeper for fish* (see fig. 19)

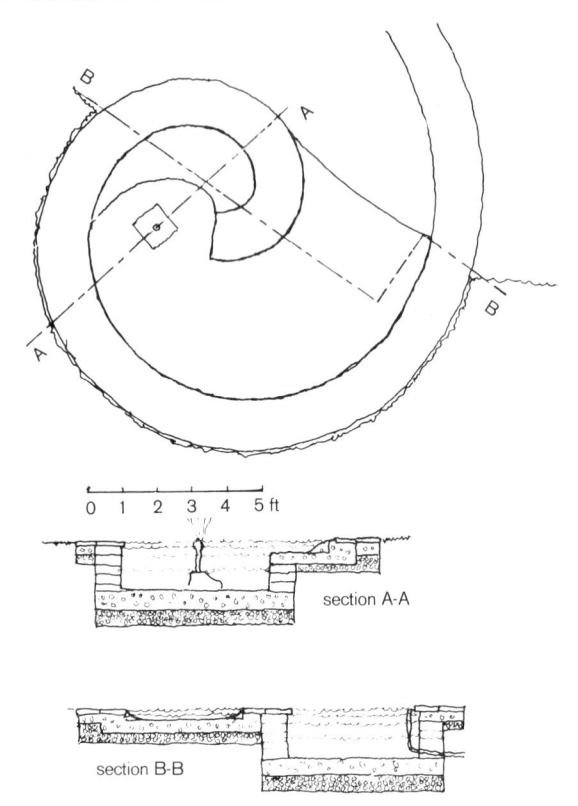

Fig. 19. *Plan and sections of the ammonite-shaped pool in pl. 62. On the left-hand side of section B–B is the bird splash, much shallower than the rest of the pool*

## Pools with plants

Reflecting pools are designed to be seen from a distance. Most garden pools are meant to be looked at from close to; as well as reflections on the surface, there may be the movements of fish below the water to look at, or just the bottom of the pool: in Spain and other hot countries pools are often lined with patterned tiles. These can be bought here (see p. 184), but they are expensive and would be wasted in a pool filled with plants. However, the bottom of a concrete pool can easily be made more interesting by setting pebbles or shells into the concrete before it is set, either at random or in a pattern.

Stone and concrete (see p. 174) were for many years the standard materials for pool linings, with puddled clay for the bottom when it was available, as in Le Nôtre's great pools at Fontainebleau. Today there are also plastics, which are much cheaper and easier to handle.

The moulded glass fibre pools sold by most garden centres are somewhat stiff and artificial in shape and limited in scope. Greater freedom of shape can be had by laying your own pool with sheet plastics obtainable from garden centres and some builders' merchants. Polythene is too fragile for a permanent pool. PVC brands like Butylite (with a fifty-year guarantee), Lotylite, Flexilene and Juralene are more reliable. Nurseries specializing in water gardens (Highlands Water Gardens and Stapely Water Gardens, addresses on p. 183) who also supply the PVC, give illustrated laying instructions in their catalogues. Basic construction details are given on pp. 166 – 7. Try not to make a hard line with the stones if you want an informal pool. Turf can also be used to cover the plastic overlap, except where a bank slopes steeply to the water's edge, in which case the turf will gradually wash away, leaving the plastic exposed to view.

## *PLANTING*

If the pool is not in a paved area, you may want to grow plants as close to it as possible, choosing the kind of plants that grow beside a natural pool, like marsh marigolds or *Iris kaempferi*, which like very moist ground. But the soil round a plastic pool is as dry as the rest of the garden. It is wiser to choose plants that *look* like moisture-lovers, such as *Iris sibirica*, rhubarb (*Rheum palmatum*) and plantain lilies (hostas), which can survive with normal watering.

A pool in which it is proposed to grow water lilies and other aquatics should have sun for at least half the day – longer if possible. The more sun, the more flowers. Unfortunately, green algae and blanket weed also thrive in sunlight. Trying to get rid of them by chemical means is not recommended, especially where there are fish. Green algae can be skimmed off with a net and blanket weed pulled out by hand, but the best plan is to try to establish a balanced ecology, with fish, plants, underwater oxygenating plants (see list, p. 89) and scavengers like water snails and water-fleas (Daphnia) keeping things under control. Specialist nurseries will generally advise on this. It is partly a question of experiment followed by good maintenance, and makes the pool more interesting, especially for children. A small fountain jet can also help by keeping the water moving, but water lilies dislike too much disturbance. For a more drastic treatment, see pp. 178–9.

The depth of a pool depends on what plants are to grow in it. The largest water lilies need two to three feet of water; the smallest will make do with six to twelve inches; so will floating aquatics like the water hyacinth (*Eichhornia*). Water lilies can be planted in soil on the bottom of the pool or in baskets or polythene pots (Highland Water Gardens; Stapely Water Gardens).

Another group of plants prefers to grow in soil below water level at the side of the pool (see list on p. 88). For these, a trough like that illustrated in fig. 20 should be made, although they have been known to succeed in a small milk crate lined with grass turves. The

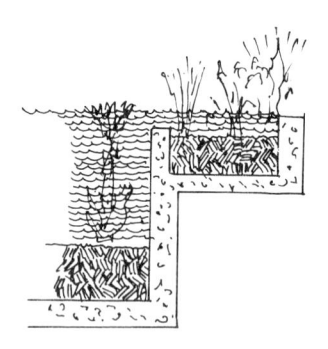

Fig. 20. *Section showing an underwater planting trough at the side of a pool, for plants that grow with their feet in water. The outer edge of the trough is below water level, but high enough to prevent soil from washing away*

63. *Waterside planting of* Hosta fortunei, Rodgersia pinnata *and hydrangeas. The striped grass growing in the water is* Scirpus zebrinus

important point to remember is that the top of the container should be below the surface of the water, but high enough to prevent the soil it contains from being washed away. Like the water lilies, these plants should be planted in early summer.

Suburban gardeners lucky enough to be on a river or have a natural pool can cultivate another group of plants – those that like very moist soil (see p. 89).

## FOUNTAINS

For hundreds of years fountains were a pleasure reserved for the very rich or those lucky enough to have a natural supply of water at high level to provide the necessary gravity force. The submersible pump has changed all that. Today, the murmur of fountain jets is heard in countless gardens, no matter how small.

A fountain is at its most spectacular when it comes between you and the sun, because it breaks up the water into a thousand tiny drops that sparkle like diamonds, constantly changing as they catch the light. So the position should be chosen with care. If it is to be

## Town Gardens to Live In

lit up at night, it should also be visible from the windows. Small jets are generally operated by a submersible electric pump from inside the pool. The height can be varied by a valve regulating the water flow. A higher jet needs a more powerful pump, larger pipes (up to one inch, according to the size of the jet) and a larger nozzle. The size of a jet and the angle at which it shoots into the air depends on the size of the nozzle and its position in relation to the water surface. One type of nozzle just below the surface produces the unusual whirlpool effect seen in pl. 64.

A pump used by many gardeners is the Otter, made in several sizes and obtainable at most large hardware stores. It is not expensive, costs very little to run (just over a penny an hour for the small size) and circulates the same water round and round. The pool itself is filled and kept topped up by hosepipe. The pump, which sits in the pool, has a length of waterproof electric cable built into it and is normally supplied with a waterproof connector. This must be housed in an easily accessible, protected place near the edge of the pool above ground – a small chamber, of a few bricks covered by a paving slab and floored with gravel to ensure that any moisture drains away; a plastic sandwich box can often be adapted to serve the same purpose. From the connector to the house it is necessary to use a heavy duty waterproof electric cable designed for outdoor use. This should be carried below ground in

64. *Whirlpool fountains at the RHS Wisley gardens*

*65. An easily maintained garden of fountain jets that is safe for children, in Washington, USA*

an alkathene tube or hosepipe which will help to keep it dry and protected. It should run beneath the lawn, a path or the stone edging to a bed, to protect it from accidental damage while digging. If you must carry it beneath cultivated ground, bury it below spade depth and cover the tube with a row of bricks or run it through some terracotta land-drain pipes to avoid accidents.

Two kinds of lighting systems can be obtained from garden centres: low voltage underwater Aquaglow kits (12 volts) or Moonglow garden kits (18 volts), made by Lotus Water Garden Products; and high voltage Lotus mains lighting units (150 volts), which are more expensive.

## CASCADES

To get the maximum effect, a cascade should face the sun. Its sparkle is increased if the edge of the stone over which the water falls is fluted or roughly finished. A smoother cascade, as in pl. 66, is produced by the water falling over a projecting lip of concrete or stone, or over a slightly curved metal sheet laid on top of the stone edge and grouted into the side walls. The volume of water should be sufficient to fill the opening through which it pours, otherwise it will just trickle over, leaving green stains on the stones. If this happens after you have made the cascade, you must invent some way of reducing the size of the opening. Artificial cascades are

66. *Pool and cascade at Stuttgart, Germany*

operated by the same kind of pump as the fountain jets. Some pumps will operate cascades and fountains at the same time.

The sound of a cascade is to some people as important as the sight. The garden in pl. 60 has an almost invisible cascade that flows all the year round except in frosty weather, just for the sake of the sound. The tone can be regulated when the cascade is made, according to the height of the drop (the bigger the drop, the louder and lower the tone), and whether the water falls in one piece (deep) or is broken up as it falls (light).

If the sun will always be behind the cascade (in a north-falling garden, for instance), it is worth considering a device which comes from India, where it was much used by the Mughul emperors. It is a *chadar* (which means sheet) – a slab of stone tilted at an angle of

67. *A cascade of home-made pre-cast concrete slabs, slightly hollowed in the centre. In the foreground, an underwater planting trough*

68. *A* chadar, *or ripple cascade, in Lahore*

69. *An English cascade inspired by the Mughul cascade; it is made of short lengths of angle-iron embedded in reconstructed stone*

Town Gardens to Live In

about thirty degrees so that it catches the light from any angle (pl. 68). The carved surface causes the water to gleam and chuckle as it ripples down. It could be made in concrete or fired clay, with a pattern of your own design carved on it while the concrete was still soft.

## Some plants for pools

### Floating leaves and flowers

Floating water hyacinth with lavender-blue flowers (*Eichhornia crassipes* Major); frog-bit (*Hydrocharis morsus-ranae*), like a tiny water lily; water chestnut (*Trapa natans*) with white flowers; water lilies (*Nymphea*) in a variety of sizes and colours.

### Pool-side plants growing in water

American water plantain (*Alisma parviflora*), white flowers; arrow arum (*Peltandra virginica*), white flowers; arrowhead (*Sagittaria sagittifolia*, *S. graminea*, etc.), white flowers; bog arum (*Calla palustris*), white flowers; bulrush (*Scirpus lacustris*); flowering rush

70. *Variegated* Iris laevigata *at the sides of a pool at the RHS Wisley gardens*

# Water

(*Butomus umbellatus*), pink flowers; *Pontederia cordata*, blue flowers; sweet flag (*Acorus calamus*), fragrant leaves; water iris (*Iris laevigata*), several varieties; yellow water iris (*Iris pseudacorus*), large plant; zebra rush (*Scirpus zebrinus*), grass with horizontal stripes.

*Underwater oxygenators*

*Callitriche autumnalis*; *Elodea canadensis*, inclined to ramp; *Ranunculus aquatilis*; *Tillaea recurva*, good food for fish; water celery (*Apium inundatum*), small white flowers above water; water violet (*Hottonia palustris*), flowers violet-white.

*For wet soil beside the pool*

*Cyperus vegetus*, grass-like; day lilies (*Hemerocallis*), many varieties; gardener's garters (*Phalaris arundinacea* Picta), a striped grass; *Gunnera manicata*, very large; *Iris kaempferi*, several varieties; *Ligularia clivorum*, orange flowers; *Lysichitum americanum*, like giant spinach, yellow flowers; marsh marigold (*Caltha palustris*); plantain lilies (*Hosta*), lilac or white flowers, large leaves; *Rheum palmatum*; *Smilacina racemosa*, white flowers; Solomon's seal (*Polygonatum multiflorum*), creamy flowers.

## 7  Shade and Winter

Shade and winter raise different problems, but the solution to one will often do equally well for the other. In neither case is much colour likely to be available. Form is therefore especially important, and can best be achieved by working out a framework of permanent evergreen planting, paths and paving, either geometrical or informal.

The framework of the formal garden in pl. 71 could hardly be simpler. Two rows of false acacias (*Robinia pseudoacacia*) in long rectangular beds of shade-tolerant underplanting divide the garden lengthwise into three, with a broad lawn in between. Round the outer edge runs a gravel path with more shade planting against the wall – foxgloves, cranesbills, dead nettle (*Lamium galeobdolen*); a shady garden that retains its shape in winter and needs little maintenance.

71. *A formal garden in west London. Beneath two rows of false acacias are long box-edged planting beds of* Pachysandra terminalis *with occasional cross-bands of variegated hebe*

72. *A garden with a formal pattern. Eight different varieties of box have have been used to create an all-the-year-round garden that would also be suitable for a shady situation*

Box, one of the best plants for shade and winter, is more versatile than is generally realized. The small garden illustrated in pl. 72 uses eight different varieties: as a climber up the walls, in a low formal ground pattern, and to create a composition of solids and voids. In this garden, bamboo is used as a solid screen along one wall, held in place by a strong chain taken down once a year so that new shoots can be gathered in and enclosed before the chain is replaced. Clipped box can be treated as minor architecture and used to enclose small spaces. In pl. 73 it has been clipped into curved recesses filled with ivy. Since box is a slow grower, a box garden is for someone who expects to live in the same house for several years. Some varieties are slower than others, so check in a good nursery catalogue.

These two gardens are based on traditional designs. The Danish garden in pl. 74 belongs to today. With a minimum of fuss, and using very ordinary materials, its designer has created an abstract composition that is barely affected by seasonal changes. The planting is almost entirely of conifers: these could be chosen from slow-growing or dwarf varieties: *Pinus mugo pumilio*, *Picea abies* Clanbrassiliana, *Juniperus* Pfitzeriana and *J. sabina* Tamariscifolia, *Cedrus libani* Nana and the slightly larger blue spruce, *Picea pungens* Glauca or another of the same group. Semi-prostrate yews might

73. *A path at Colonial Williamsburg, USA, enclosed by clipped box and ivy*

also be suitable. Conifers do badly in heavily polluted air – shrubs can be used instead: evergreen cotoneasters (*C. glaucophyllus* or *C. salicifolius* Rugosus with graceful arching branches), or the rounded shapes of rhododendrons and elaeagnus. The basic idea of using a decorative wall as a backcloth for evergreens can be developed in a number of ways, ranging from an arrangement of concrete units as in pls. 53 and 54 to the simple contrast between a whitened wall or painted trellis and the solid dark green of viburnums, rhododendrons or camellias.

Not all evergreens have dark foliage. The young leaves of *Pieris forrestii* and *P. japonica* Bert Chandler are bright red, changing to

74. *An arrangement of walls, fence and conifers that provides interest, whatever the season, in a Danish garden*

## Shade and Winter

cream and finally pale green; *Elaeagnus pungens* Maculata and *E. p.* Variegata have yellow variegated markings; fatsias, griselinias, skimmias and Balearic Island box (*Buxus balearica*) are bright green; *Senecio greyi* is silvery; *Garrya elliptica* has greyish leaves and jade green catkins in winter. Ivies, a most useful ground cover, vary greatly in colour; some have white or cream markings. The colour contrasts provided by some deciduous shrubs (see p. 32) will also add brightness to shady gardens, though they do not help in winter. For contrasts of form there are mahonias, bamboos, New Zealand flax (*Phormium tenax*), including one with vertical yellow stripes, and spiky yuccas. Here, for example, is the planting list of a small dark courtyard garden in Hatfield New Town: Pampas grass (*Cortaderia selloana*), two different laurels (*Prunus laurocerasus* Schipkaensis with broad leaves, *P. l.* Zabeliana with narrow ones), *Fatsia japonica*, bamboo (*Arundinaria murieliae*), *Cotoneaster horizontalis*, yellow broom (for its foliage), *Juniperus virginiana* Grey Owl and an evergreen ceanothus (also for foliage), with ground cover of *Hypericum calycinum* and the variegated form of *Pachysandra terminalis*.

## *SHADE*

One beneficial effect of shade in a small garden is that it gives a sense of depth – exactly what such gardens need. Outlines and distances become indistinct, leaving room for the mind to expand. Where shade is cast by trees and not by buildings, the light that filters through the leaves is soft and flickering; in winter, the branches throw dramatic shadows on the ground.

Few gardens are in perpetual shade all over: usually at least one corner is reached by the sun, if only for a short time. The garden in pl. 77 is almost completely overshadowed in summer by a magnificent old chestnut tree, but in the late afternoon one corner is clear of shade. Here, for an hour or so, a strategically placed golden elder (*Sambucus nigra* Aurea) glows with light. Another opportunity comes in spring, before the chestnut leaves shut out the sun. Early bulbs fill small beds left in the paving round the tree trunk; later, the beds are taken over by *Campanula poscharskyana*,

75. *Planting for the shady side of a garden. Reading from right to left: pale creamy leaves of* Pieris forrestii, *evergreen azaleas, camellias, white-edged leaves of* Hosta decorata *Thomas Hogg,* Spirea × arguta *Bridal Wreath,* Viburnum tormentosum *Mariesii (white flowers), grey-green* Garrya elliptica. *The sun only touches the tops of the plants for a short time on a summer morning*

76. *A shady walk: against the wall on the right are camellias and ivies; on the left, variegated ivies, hostas, striped gardener's garters and* Kerria japonica *Variegata.*

Shade and Winter

which has to be thinned out in autumn to give the bulbs a chance.

As well as making the most of existing opportunities, you can bring more light into your garden in a number of ways. The two most effective are a light colour-wash on the walls (see p. 72) and a shallow pool large enough to reflect the sky (see p. 77). Planting can also help: not only shrubs with variegated foliage (p. 32) and smaller herbaceous plants like hostas, several of which have cream or white markings, but also flowers with pale colours. Deep crimsons and purples almost disappear in shade (this also applies to gardens with one shady and one sunny side, where dark colours show up better on the sunny side). And though you may not be able to bring the light down to the plants, you can do the reverse by planting in raised beds. Two feet or so makes a surprising difference.

When a garden is dank as well as dark, look for the reason. Perhaps dense overhanging foliage is preventing air from reaching the garden and ought to be thinned or cut back. Or the soil may need better drainage. This can be cured by digging down for about a foot (setting the topsoil on one side) and putting in six to eight inches of fine rubble before replacing the topsoil.

77. *A golden elder planted where it will catch the late afternoon sun in a garden shaded by an old chestnut tree*

78. *Light catches the leaves of a rhubarb* (Rheum palmatum) *on the shady side of a south London garden*

## More plants for shade

### Shrubs

Full shade: *Azalea, Hamamelis* (witch hazel), *Hypericum, Ilex* (holly), *Kalmia, Kerria, Laurus nobilis* (bay), *Mahonia, Philadelphus* (some), *Pieris, Pyracantha* (firethorn), *Rhododendron, Ribes* (flowering currant), *Rubus* (ornamental bramble), *Sarcococca, Skimmia, Stranvaesia, Symphoricarpos* (snowberry), *Vinca major* (periwinkle).

Half shade: *Berberis, Cotoneaster, Daphne, Fuchsia, Hydrangea, Osmanthus, Potentilla, Rodgersia, Senecio, Spiraea, Viburnum, Weigela.*

### Herbaceous, etc.

Full shade: *Anemone* (including Japanese anemones), *Bergenia,* bluebell, *Brunnera macrophylla, Digitalis* (foxglove), ferns, *Geranium* (cranesbill), hellebore, *Hosta, Polygonum, Primula, Pulmonaria, Solidago* (golden rod), *Tradescantia.*

Half shade: *Acanthus, Aconitum, Aquilegia, Astilbe, Astrantia, Campanula, Doronicum, Hemerocallis* (day lily), *Ligularia, Monarda* (bergamot), *Myosotis* (forget-me-not), *Oenothera* (evening primrose), peony, *Tellima.*

### Low ground cover

*Asperula odorata* (sweet woodruff – quick-spreading), *Convallaria majalis* (lily of the valley), *Epimedium, Fragaria* (alpine strawberry – half-shade), *Geranium macrorrhizum, Heuchera brizoides, Lamium maculatum* and *L. galeobdolon* (quick-spreading), *Omphalodes verna, Pachysandra terminalis, Polygonum vaccinifolium, Saxifraga umbrosa* (London pride), *Tiarella cordifolia* (foam flower), *Vinca minor* (small periwinkle).

# WINTER

The general feeling seems to be that in winter we should be thankful for small mercies. But there is nothing insignificant about the

79. *Ferns*, Hosta undulata, Geranium sanguineum lancastriense, *a variegated hebe and two varieties of mind your own business, one with golden foliage, in a dark corner of a London garden*

clouds of white or pink blossom that the winter-flowering cherry (*Prunus subhirtella* Autumnalis) produces, lasting for several weeks in mild weather. And a surprising number of trees and shrubs flower between December and February, given the right conditions (see pp. 99–100). Of course, the most beautiful effects of all are beyond

80. *The garden in pl. 59 (p. 77) under snow*

*81. Tree shadows on the snow*

our control: the delicate white edging of frost round the leaves of evergreens, the shadow of a tree on newly fallen snow. Snow rests in different ways on paving and foliage. The paving and the ground pattern are more clearly defined, the foliage is given a new shape and the structure of plants is emphasized. Plants with leathery leaves are more likely to break under the weight of snow. Feathery ones will bend and eventually spring back to their original positions.

Foremost among the pleasures of the garden in winter are the shapes of trees and their trunks: the silky brown bark of *Prunus serrula* and other cherries; the rough white or pinkish trunks of certain birches (*Betula caerulea-grandis*, *B. jacquemontii* or *B. albo-sinensis*); snake-bark and paperbark maples (*Acer grosseri* and *A. griseum*); the silver-grey of the catalpa. Most willows are too large for small gardens, but room can be found in a medium-sized suburban garden for *Salix chrysocoma* with its golden cascade of twigs.

Shrubs that contribute to winter colour are dogwoods with bright red or yellow stems (*Cornus alba* and *C. a.* Sibirica, *C. stolonifera* Flaviramea); *Salix alba* Britzensis (syn. Chermesina) with bright coppery branches; the strange white stems of two ornamental brambles (*Rubus biflorus* and *R. cockburnianus*); and an impressive array of berries – on the ground, up the walls or hanging from above – from the cotoneaster family and many others.

Some ground-cover plants are at their most colourful in winter. The leaves of *Bergenia* Evening Glow turn to copper: *Euonymus*

82. *A winter scene: the silver-grey trunk of a catalpa, New Zealand flax and box*

*fortunei* Variegatus becomes tinged with lilac; and the variegated form of bugle (*Ajuga reptans* Variegata) takes on a pink glow, making an interesting contrast with the bronzy purple form.

## Some mid-winter flowers

### December

Trees: *Prunus subhirtella* Autumnalis.
Shrubs: *Erica carnea, Hamamelis mollis, Jasminum nudiflorum, Lonicera fragrantissima, Mahonia media, Viburnum bodnantense* and *V. tinus.*
Herbaceous perennials: *Helleborus niger* and *H. n.* Macranthus (Christmas rose).

### January

Trees: *Acacia dealbata.*
Shrubs: *Camellia sasanqua, Chimonanthus praecox* (winter sweet),

## Town Gardens to Live In

*Erica carnea* and *E. darleyensis*, *Garrya elliptica*, *Hamamelis mollis*, *Jasminum nudiflorum*, *Lonicera standishii*, *Sarcococca* (various), *Viburnum bodnantense*, *V. farreri* and *V. tinus*.

Herbaceous perennials, etc.: *Helleborus niger*, *H. orientalis* (Lenten rose) and *H. viridis* (green hellebore), *Iris unguicularis* [*stylosa*].

*February*

Trees: *Acacia dealbata*, *Prunus conradinae*, *P. davidiana*, *P. incisa* Praecox and *P. mume*, *Rhododendron arboreum*, *Sorbus megalocarpa*.
Shrubs: *Camellia sasanqua*, *Cornus mas*, *Daphne mezereum* and *D. odora*, *Mahonia japonica*, *Pachysandra terminalis*, *Rhododendron dauricum* and *R. mucronulatum*, *Ulex europaeus* (gorse), and all in the January list except winter sweet.

Herbaceous perennials, etc.: *Anemone hepatica*, *Eranthis* (winter aconite), *Helleborus orientalis*, *H. corsicus* and *H. viridis*, *Iris unguicularis* and *Scilla bifolia* (two-leaved squill).

## 8 Planning for Easy Maintenance

Some people put easy maintenance before everything else. There are those who like to be surrounded by plants but do not enjoy gardening or have no time for it. Others like gardening but are physically unable to do much stooping or heavy work.

The design requirements of the two differ, but they have one thing in common – the need to start off with soil that is in good condition, since it will probably get less turning over than in an ordinary garden. A small area of earth, especially when surrounded by paving, can soon become exhausted and sour from lack of aeration.

This is one of the most difficult problems for town gardeners. Bringing in new soil is very expensive – a last resort in desperate cases. Farmyard manure is unobtainable, unless you happen to live near a riding stable, which may be glad to sell at a reasonable price (but it must be given time to rot down). Peat and sand help to

83. *A small paved garden in Denmark*

84. *Planting that looks after itself in a London garden (bamboos, giant hogweed, hydrangeas, azaleas, rhododendrons and hebes)*

lighten heavy soil, but the best remedy is a slow-acting fertilizer like bonemeal or basic slag, which release their contents over several years. A yearly mulch of leaf mould (obtainable from some nurseries) or, better still, your own compost (see p. 164) will greatly improve soil which has dried out – a frequent cause of plant failure, particularly in town gardens.

The easiest garden to look after is one that is paved throughout, with small gaps for permanent planting. It is not dependent on annuals or bedding out, but relies solely on beautiful foliage and plant form. Controlling the plants and cleaning their leaves with a hose to which a rose has been fitted is almost the only summer gardening needed; in autumn, there are just the dead leaves to sweep up. A stand-pipe concealed behind a bush makes watering easy.

Such treatment is only suitable for small areas. Larger gardens must be tackled differently. Pl. 84 shows a shady London garden in which the main planting interest is concentrated near the house and

## Planning for Easy Maintenance

has been encouraged to become so dense that after three years it is self-maintaining. A small footbridge from the house, crossing a basement area, introduces an architectural note which is reinforced by the strong forms of the plants: giant hogweed (*Heracleum mantegazzianum*), two bamboos (one the small-leaved *Arundinaria murieliae*), rhododendrons, hydrangeas, ceanothus, yellow azaleas, hebes, roses and a white lilac. Except for a paved sitting area against the far wall, the rest of the garden is grassed; luckily, mowing is no great chore with an electric mower. If, when the garden is made, a slow-growing grass with a high proportion of fine-leaved sheep's fescue is sown (seed from W. W. Johnson, Boston, Lincs., or Sutton's Summer Day), the number of cuts required in a season is reduced. A further aid to mowing, where grass is enclosed by planting, is a stone edge to the flower-beds (pl. 85) – this allows the plants to spread out without getting in the way of the mower.

Ground cover dense enough to smother weeds is another labour-saver and makes a good setting for larger plants. It takes at least two years to get established. After that, some control should be exercised about once a year. Certain plants can take over completely if left to themselves. In a sunny position, creeping thyme (*Thymus serpyllum*) will soon cover a large area. More serious is the invasive habit of the variegated dead nettle *Lamium galeobdolen*, a beautiful ramper that is invaluable for shady areas but is best planted on its own in a confined space. It should be clipped over in April to get

85. *Stone edging separates lawn and plants*

86. *Ground cover of creeping thyme* (Thymus serpyllum) *on the left of the picture flows round the larger plants:* Clerodendrum trichotomum, *peonies,* Stachys lanata, *kniphofia*

a good variegated effect. A number of ground-cover plants have already been mentioned (p. 31), but a much wider range will be found in specialist books (see p. 181).

Raised beds, not less than two feet above ground level, make gardening easier for those who dislike stooping (pls. 87 and 88). Make sure that they have good drainage (see fig. 21) and if they are to stand on a hard surface (in a roof garden, for instance), they should have small weep-holes just above ground level. The width is important: you should be able to reach all parts of the bed without undue stretching. The island bed in pl. 87 can be reached from all sides, and is about six feet wide. In positions where trees or hedges take all the goodness out of the soil, a raised bed has the advantage that the soil is separate and remains unaffected.

Various materials can be used to make retaining walls for raised beds. In pl. 87 it is precast concrete with a coarse dark green aggregate, mitred at the corners (a skilled operation); in pl. 88, precast concrete with shuttering of old railway sleepers; in fig. 21 plain concrete slabs have been used, but stone would do equally well. Brick is visually a softer material and also more absorbent, so that it can be sprayed with water to help combat evaporation in hot weather. Only very thick timber is suitable; other kinds quickly rot.

87. *Raised bed with sides of pre-cast concrete with a coarse dark green aggregate. The lower part of the retaining wall is recessed to give room for the gardener's toes*

If labour-saving is important, the very idea of a clipped hedge will be rejected out of hand. Remember that although clipping the sides is not a heavy task, keeping the top trimmed needs more effort; unless you are careful to keep it below five feet, sooner or

88. *Raised bed with concrete sides in front of a yew hedge; old railway sleepers were used for the shuttering*

Town Gardens to Live In

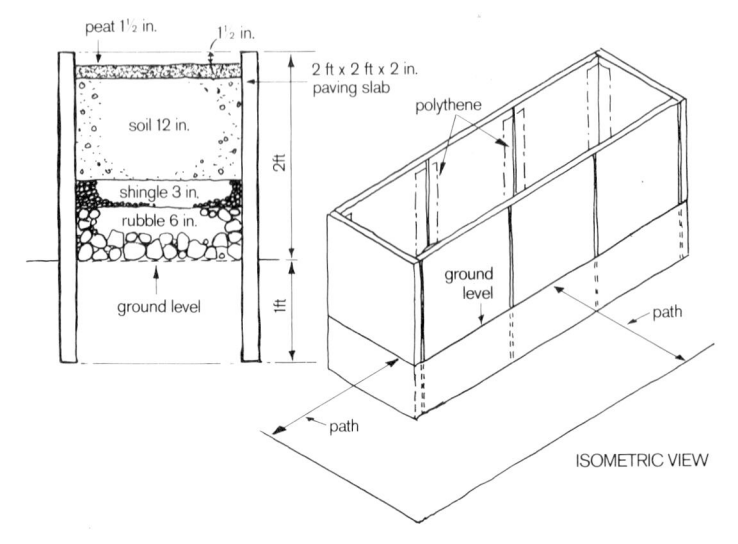

Fig. 21. *Section and isometric view of a raised bed with concrete slabs. It is high enough for the disabled or the blind to garden in comfort*

later you will have to stand on a ladder to do the job properly. If you really want a hedge, avoid privet, which needs several cuts in a summer. Choose beech, hornbeam, holly or yew (except in polluted air) – these only need one. Or have an informal untrimmed hedge of berberis or escallonia.

Climbing roses are not for those who are nervous of climbing ladders, as they may need high-level pruning after only two or three seasons. But there are many lovely bush roses, and perhaps your neighbour's roses will climb over the wall to console you.

## 9 *Sitting Space*

Victoria Sackville-West, who wrote *In Your Garden*, one of the great gardening books, once painted an amusing word picture of her mother whiling away many happy hours sitting muffled to the ears in the snow at Knole: sometimes she even had her meals on the terrace. Few fresh-air enthusiasts would go to such extremes. As a nation, we spend more and more time in the open, but we like to do so in comfort. So what are the points to watch?

The position of an outdoor room will depend on the sun. But a sitting space directly linked with the house is more useful than one at the other end of the garden – for sitting out to shell peas, for the occasional cup of coffee on a sunny spring morning, or for children's play. It also acts more effectively as an extension to the house: in the Islington garden in pls. 89 and 90 and fig. 22 the main living-room and the tiny garden are treated as one space. Only a wide sheet of glass separates the two, and the sense of unity is heightened by reflections of the garden in a long mirror on the wall facing the window.

An outdoor room should be dry underfoot if it is to be usable in unsettled weather and not reserved for heatwaves. Stone or concrete paving with mortared joints gives a firm and even surface for tables and chairs. Brick is less satisfactory unless laid with professional skill. Cobbles, setts and gravel are too rough in texture. The size of the paved area will vary according to what is available, but if people are not to feel cramped, certain minimum sizes should be borne in mind: for two people, about 6 ft × 6 ft or its equivalent (4 ft × 9 ft, for example); for six to eight people, 12 ft × 12 ft.

Protection from draughts is essential, either by a hedge (see pp. 69–71) or a screen. If a screen, the overall effect will be more harmonious if it is in some way related to the architecture of the house, possibly echoing the pattern or shape of the windows (pl. 91). Provision should also be made for shade if there is no

89
90

## Sitting Spaces

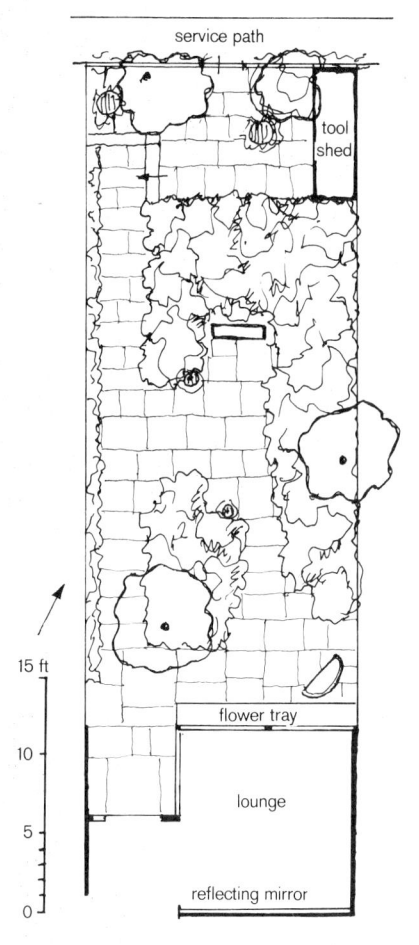

Fig. 22. *Plan of a small paved garden in Islington. It is treated as an extension of the ground floor of the house, with two sitting areas. Through the wide window the garden flows into the living-room and is reflected in a mirror on the opposite wall. The tool shed, neatly fitted in beside the gate to the service path, is hidden by planting*

convenient tree. Timber slats with metal supports will quickly be covered by vines, clematis or other climbers that give dappled shade (pl. 92), and make an interesting permanent feature. Or an overhead canopy can be made out of some light material like

*Pl. 89 looks out at the garden across the back of a settee, with a broad window ledge for flowerpots in front. Pl. 90, taken from near the house door, shows one of the two sitting spaces*

109

91. *A paved sitting area enclosed by a screen which echoes the windows of the house*

92. *A pergola of white wooden slats with black metal supports, soon to be covered by vines*

93. *Riviera fencing across the top of the sitting area casts interesting shadows. It can be rolled into position when needed. A length of the same fencing has been fixed to the wall* (see p. 184)

Riviera fencing (split bamboos threaded together), to be kept rolled up at one side, about seven feet above ground level; when needed, it is unfurled by hand so that it rests on wires that stretch across the sitting space (pl. 93).

One of the great pleasures of sitting in a garden is to feel oneself surrounded by growing things, with the scent of alyssum, cistus, mock orange and the like all about one. Planting should therefore be brought right up to the paved area, at least in places, and there should be no rigid dividing line (pl. 94). Large pots can be kept permanently on the paving, some filled with shrubs, others with bulbs and bedding plants; smaller pots of seasonal plants like lilies

94. *Planting comes right up to the sitting area, which has a built-in stone bench round the walls*

95. *A secluded breakfast area catching the morning sun*

96. *A clematis-covered arbour on a stone platform, beyond the reach of the shadow cast by a north-facing house*

97. *A communal sitting area on a housing estate at Milton Keynes*

98. *Fibreglass furniture by Grosfillex*

99. *Stone furniture in a Danish garden*

100. *A built-in barbecue*

## Sitting Spaces

or fuchsias can be added as and when they come into flower, and returned to their normal protected position when they finish. Fibreglass pots are useful for this, because they weigh so little. A list of suggestions for pot planting is given on pp. 151–3.

Fibreglass is also useful for garden furniture. Besides being light, it can be left out of doors until summer is over (pl. 98). Well-painted metal furniture is nearly as rain resistant, especially if welded rather than bolted. Stone furniture has the great merit of being out at all times – but needs a cushion.

A barbecue is the latest addition to summer in the garden. The obvious place for it is the sitting space – the focal point of family life in warm weather, especially if it has outdoor lighting. Portable barbecues are not expensive, but built-in ones are more stable and always available, like stone furniture. The barbecue in pl. 100 is well placed near the edge of the paved area and is built of the same material as the garden wall, so that it fits smoothly into the general background. More elaborate versions can become design features in their own right.

101. *Barbecue*

## 10  Children

Children enjoy gardens as much as their parents but as they grow, their exuberance can pose problems. With foresight of things to come, gardens can, however, be planned to grow with the children. Beautifully manicured gardens and children are not compatible, but a compromise can be made.

A small baby in a pram placed under a tree in the garden will take pleasure in watching the dancing leaves and the play of light. Toddlers, unsteady on their feet, but bursting with curiosity and eager for new experiences, like the feel of different textures under bare feet – grass, level paving, coarse brick paths. They need space to run around, and a sand-pit near enough to the house for parents to keep a watchful eye. If possible, it should be in an open sunny position with water to hand. It should be about eighteen inches deep, with a bottom of paving-stones, laid dry, with two-inch open joints to allow for drainage. Place the stones on nine inches of rough material – gravel, broken bricks or stones – to act as a soak-

102. *A shallow paddling pool, with a sand beach and shingle. When not in use as a pool, the water is drained away and the grown-ups take possession with their garden chairs*

## Children

away. A paved surround makes a useful surface for turning out sand-pies. Cats can foul sand unless it is protected by a light movable frame covered with wide mesh chicken wire. Sand should never be entirely closed in with a solid lid for it is the sun and weather that keep it sweet. When the sand-pit is no longer needed it can be paved over as a sitting space or hopscotch pitch, or turned into a herb garden.

Water to dabble in is as attractive as sand at this age, but pools of more than a few inches deep can be dangerous. In one Danish garden, planned for children, this hazard was overcome by fixing a five-foot high water pipe, topped by a whirling spray, in the middle of a shallow concrete dish at ground level. When the tap was turned on inside the house a gentle rain fell into the pool and drained away through the plug-hole (either into a soakaway or to the main drainage). The children delighted in leaping about in the gentle shower and catching the spray in small buckets to mix with sand or to water the plants. In this way stagnant water was avoided and there was no risk of drowning. When the children were older the sunken bowl was turned into a lily pond with a central fountain jet in place of the taller pipe.

A few inches of water covering large rounded pebbles set in concrete (pl. 102) makes an attractive place for small children to paddle in. The pebble pool is filled with a hose and has a plug-hole for emptying. Close at hand is a sand beach and some washed shingle for sunbathing. Both are contained in their separate compartments by a low stone wall. This arrangement comes near to reproducing pleasures of the seaside.

Small children enjoy sitting on a low timber bench – no more than fifteen inches high – especially if there is a wide table in front for books and paintings, toys and puzzles and an occasional feast. Both should be tough enough to withstand being climbed over or camped under. If the low bench is extended in length it will be popular for crawling along.

Trees strong enough for climbing are rare in small gardens. A smooth dead tree trunk with stout branches cut to curtail its span can sometimes be obtained from the local Parks Department. This, set in a bed of concrete, can be a substitute. Later, when the

103–4. *A roof garden converted into a children's play area, with a wicker swing suspended from overhead beams, benches to climb along and a small pool*

climbing phase has passed, it can be clothed with a strong-growing rose, such as Albertine, or a clematis, planted on the shady side as it will grow towards the light.

After five years of age the problems of protecting precious plants will increase. At this stage it is better to forget the plants and think only of the children. Tricycles and scooters will be ridden at high speed round the garden. Curved undulating tracks that meander through shrubs and long grass, with small ramps at changes of level, make the ride more exciting and do far less damage. They can also be used, after the children's bedtime, for an evening stroll.

105. *A climbing tree in a Washington garden*

This is the age, too, when children delight in hiding away in secret places. Some tough quick-growing bushes (bamboos or purple osiers -- *Salix purpurea*) can be planted in advance at the end of the garden away from the house, to be developed later on, perhaps, as a wild garden thickly underplanted with bulbs and woodland flowers.

Homes for animal pets may be needed at some stage, preferably not far from the house to make feeding easy. Some pets are useful in the garden: hedgehogs eat slugs, and rabbits in an escape-proof pen can help keep the grass short. Fish ponds are a source of continuing interest, and a twelve-year-old child will probably also enjoy helping to make the pool. The finished pool should have a removable cover of wire mesh to protect the occupants from cats.

Space for football and cricket is usually only possible in larger suburban gardens. Enterprising parents in north London built,

106. *A tricycle track that is also a pleasant path round the garden*

107. *Part of the same track. Changes of level make cycling more exciting but they must be well thought out*

108. *A pierced brick wall to kick footballs against. The height has been reduced from its original 3ft 6in. since the children grew up*

# Children

109. *A secret corner behind the drooping branches of a weeping willow*

with the help of their two sons, a pierced brick wall about 3 ft 6 in. high, with a net behind it slung between two trees. If no trees are available, two strong posts will do. When the boys knocked down parts of the wall it was their job to rebuild it. Turf that got damaged by cricket was replaced by grass grown in seed boxes. During this period it is pointless to try to grow the larger herbaceous plants; alternatives are shrubs such as rugosa roses or those with whippy stems, of which there is a large selection, including forsythia, *Berberis darwinii*, *Buddleia globosa* or *B. alternifolia*, *Escallonia* C. F. Ball or *E. iveyi*, or the tough Spanish gorse, *Genista hispanica*. To protect their vulnerable small greenhouse, these parents replaced the glass with perspex. Once the danger was past the glass was reset and more tender planting was possible in the flower area.

## 11 Eats

The present impulse towards growing one's own food, combined with high prices at the greengrocer, tempts town gardeners to think seriously about producing their own vegetables, especially those that are scarce and expensive in shops. Vegetables with a high nutrition value are also worth growing: peas, French and kidney beans, carrots, leeks and white runner beans store well.

The charms of a trim vegetable garden are well known, but the average town garden is generally too much in demand as an extra living space to make such a layout possible. Ingenuity is therefore called for: space must be found in all sorts of unlikely places. The results can be astonishingly rewarding, as earlier generations of gardeners have found. In 1812, John Claudius Loudon, who may almost be said to have invented the town garden as we know it, recommended that ornamental beds of flowers and shrubs be mingled with others in which globe artichokes, asparagus, gooseberry and other fruit bushes were surrounded by clumps of strawberries (*Hints on the Formation of Gardens and Pleasure Grounds*).

The foliage and flowers of many vegetables can make a surprising contribution among flowers and shrubs. The beautiful thistle-like leaves of globe artichokes and their blue flowers can take their

110. *Globe artichokes, onions and an espaliered peach*

Eats

place in the flower beds or among flowering shrubs and, at the same time, provide delicious food (try Gros Vert de Laon from F. A. Secrett Ltd, Milford, Godalming). The coloured leaves of the Swiss chard or leaf beet (*Beta cicla*) are decorative grown as an isolated plant; the smallest leaves are good in salads, the larger cooked as spinach, and the fleshy white stems taste as good as asparagus. Break off a few leaves as you want them from the base of the plant, but do not strip entirely or the plant will die.

A tall and handsome plant, used by Gertrude Jekyll in some of her schemes for herbaceous borders, is sweet corn (maize). Grow it in small groups of six or eight – pollination is dependent on the wind and it is rare for single plants to be fertilized. Earth the plants up slightly as they grow, so that they are not rocked by the wind.

Leeks are especially suitable for growing in odd spots – they are not particular about position, they look decorative and do not need spraying. Unlike peas and beans, which must be eaten as soon as they are ripe, leeks can be left undisturbed throughout the winter until they are wanted.

Batavia and other special varieties of lettuce can be sown in spaces left by early-flowering annuals and can keep you supplied with salads till February. Another type of lettuce, known as 'loosehead' because it does not make a head, produces a continuous

111. *The foliage of loosehead lettuce (right) does not look out of place among pots of flowers*

112. *Runner beans growing up a hedge*

113. *The decorative leaves of runner beans seen against the light*

supply of leaves (again, do not strip to the base of the plant). It is particularly suitable for small households and can be grown in pots (pl. 111) (Grand Rapids and Salad Bowl, seed from Thompson & Morgan).

Runner beans are decorative and productive, whether climbing up walls among other plants, clothing an arch over a path, or up poles arranged as a wigwam, either in pots or in a flower bed. They need plenty of water at the roots during hot weather, to counteract transpiration from their fleshy leaves and prevent bud drop. They like protection from the wind (which discourages bees at flowering time). Don't put on too much nitrogenous manure, as it encourages too many leaves. White-flowered runner beans (Fry and White Energo) or the apricot-pink variety (Sutton's Sunset) seem to set better than the red and, to some eyes, are less discordant in colour. They have the additional advantage that the mature beans in the pod can be dried and harvested for winter use, whereas the red wither. Climbing French beans (Sutton's Earliest of All) also produce white haricot beans. If sweet peas are grown among the runner beans, bees are attracted to the flowers of the sweet peas and help to pollinate the runner beans *en route*.

The hardy perennial tree onion (*Allium cepa aggregatum*) produces small onions along its four-foot stems and on the tips – another space saver. It takes two years to mature from the planting of the bulbels. The Welsh onion (not really Welsh but Siberian) is

## Eats

another cut-and-come-again space saver. Its young sprouts are useful as spring onions and it needs no special attention except to be kept free from weeds (Laxton & Bunyard Nurseries).

Radishes, courgettes, bush marrows and outdoor cucumbers (Carter's Outdoor) will all flourish in large pots and half-tubs, side by side with flowers, and are themselves most decorative in leaf, flower and fruit (pl. 114). All these, and tomatoes too, can also be grown in bags of specially prepared soil called Gro-bags, stocked by most gardening shops. The bag can be used for about three years, although the second and third year crops may be less abundant. The bags are a rather bright colour and should be masked by small pot plants placed in front (pl. 131), though these should not be so tall as to keep the sun off the crop.

Even in a small garden space can usually be found for soft fruit. Birds seem to be attracted to the red fruits of raspberries, strawberries and red currants (which require netting), but leave blackberries and black currants untouched. Strawberries can also be grown in special pots, even in partial shade. Alpine strawberries make excellent ground cover or can be grown as an edging to the front of a planting bed; the most popular variety is Baron Solemacher. In winter, the leaves of these strawberries have a subtle scent.

There are thornless loganberries and blackberries – an important consideration for the picker – and the highly ornamental Japanese

114. *Radishes grown in a shallow pot side by side with agapanthus, geraniums and lilies*

115. *A handmade strawberry pot. It will take twenty-eight plants*

*116. Blackberries trained along a wall behind a bed of herbaceous plants which will have finished flowering when it is time to pick the fruit*

wineberry with orange fruit; all can be trained on brown Netlon which merges well with the background of wall or fence. They can also be grown alongside a path on four or five strands of strong wire (eighteen inches apart) stretched between sturdy posts. An established thornless blackberry (Denver Thornless or Oregon Thornless) can produce twenty to thirty pounds of fruit and its parsley-leaved foliage is clean and decorative. The Himalayan blackberry, although a splendid cropper of fine-flavoured fruit, can sometimes be a little too rampant for a small garden.

The decorative fruit of flowering crab apples (John Downie or Montreal Beauty) can be made into wine or jelly. The 'family'

*117. Espaliered apples beside a path*

118. *Cordon gooseberries and lettuce grow where once there was a low ornamental hedge. Instead of flowers, the concrete bowls on the terrace are planted with marrows*

apple tree, grafted with different varieties, eaters or cookers, is yet another space saver. The different varieties will pollinate each other, but a watch must be kept that one variety does not take over and throw the tree out of balance. Apples and pears grown as cordons on a single stem or as low horizontal espaliers (pl. 117) save space and make decorative divisions in the garden or along paths, with space beneath for edgings of parsley, dwarf lavender, santolina, chives or spring onions.

Some apples and pears will set fruit on their own (apples: James Grieve, Worcester Pearmain, Ellison's Orange and Laxton's

119. *Herbs grow in a built-in trough on top of a wall*

Town Gardens to Live In

Fig. 23. *A herb garden inside a kitchen, between the sloping window and the sink*

Superb; pears: Conference and Williams' Bon Chrétien). Other varieties will not set fruit unless they are cross-pollinated by a different variety in the same group (for example, Cox's Orange Pippin by James Grieve). Even the self-pollinators will yield a better crop if they are cross-pollinated.

Gooseberries lend themselves to being trained as standards on a four-foot stem which makes them easy to prune, spray and gather, or they may be grown as cordons (pl. 118). (Standards from R. Hill; dessert cordons from Blackmoor Nurseries.) The space beneath can be used for lettuce, radishes, parsley or bulbs for cutting.

All good cooks like to gather their own herbs, preferably easily to hand near the kitchen door. Most of the smaller herbs are happy in small raised beds, in pots or boxes, among flagstones or even in a shallow, well-drained trough placed inside a south- or west-facing kitchen window (fig. 23). A large earthenware pot planted with a mixture of herbs can stand and flourish on a sunny, sheltered window sill. Cuttings of bay are easily taken in July (half peat, half

120. *The formal herb garden at the back of the garden illustrated on pp. 40–41*

sharp sand) and will grow as a small shrub in a box or flowerpot, or as a clean-limbed standard among flowers. Planted in open ground and left to itself, it will become a large bush in time.

Vines trained over an arch or pergola produce an abundance of small grapes from which jelly can be made, and sometimes wine, though they are generally unsuitable for dessert. Three good varieties are: Brant (small, black grapes, red autumn foliage); Pirovano 14 (early, reddish black, prolific in a warm situation); Royal Muscadine sometimes called Chasselas Dorée (early, golden-green).

## 12 The Naturalist

Adults can enjoy their leisure in gardens, children can play in gardens, the family can be fed from the produce of gardens, so why not a garden to welcome birds, bees, insects, butterflies and moths or any other wild creature that fancies a visit or a permanent home?

Such a garden would not be formally designed, although there must be paths weaving in and out so that the plants and shrubs can be reached and the wildlife observed. Stepping-stone paths of paving, laid on sand or ash, are more attractive than concrete. One naturalist made paths of fir-cones collected on trips to the country. She always kept a sack and shovel in her car to bring back leaf-mould, for she found that the birds soon discovered whose garden was best for feeding in. She never digs her garden but allows every seedling to grow and thins out later; many unexpected treasures have found a home by this method.

Many so-called weeds are very beautiful. Some, on the other hand, like *Oxalis acetosella* (wood sorrel) or that child of Beelzebub, the ground elder, are best enjoyed on the roadside, or in places where they cannot spread and smother other plants. The Nature Conservancy ask farmers to preserve some nettles because they

121. *A pattern of stepping-stone paths winding in and out so that plants and wild life can be observed*

provide food for the caterpillars of the peacock butterfly, the small tortoiseshell, the comma and the red admiral. *Buddleia variabilis* (a lime lover) is very attractive to the big *Vanessa* butterflies of late summer, but nettles are essential for their caterpillars (eggs and larvae of butterflies from the Butterfly Farm, Sherborne, Dorset). A small patch of nettles, with their high greenfly population in May and June, also provides food for ladybirds. By July, when the nettles die, the remaining greenfly will be feeding on vegetable crops and roses; the ladybirds will follow them and take their toll, benefiting the neighbours as well as the ladybirds.

*Plants that attract butterflies*

*Alyssum benthami*; asters; *Buddleia alternifolia, B. davidii* or *B. fallowiana*; *Caryopteris clandonensis*; *Echinacea purpurea*; *Echinops ritro* (globe thistle); *Eryngium planum* (sea holly family); *Helianthus* (perennial sunflower); *Helianthemum* (rock or sun rose); honeysuckle; lavender; *Liatris spicata* (Kansas Gay Feather); lilac; marigolds; nettles; petunias; phlox; *Rhamnus frangula* (alder buckthorn); *Rosa rubiginosa* (sweetbriar), *R. rubrifolia* and *R. rugosa*; *Rubus odoratus* (bramble family); *Rudbeckia* (cone flower); sweet rocket (*Hesperis matronalis*); *Thymus serpyllum* (thyme); verbena.

# A POOL

A naturalist in Wandsworth has a small shallow pool in his garden, about two feet long and one foot wide, shaped like a twisted willow leaf, which he dug himself and lined with concrete. Although it is eighteen inches deep in the centre (for floating plants), the edges are shallow enough for birds to drink and bathe. He arrived at this shape because he found it was less likely to crack in frost, as the ice can rise up the sides of the pool. Another device is to put a block of soft wood in the water; when the ice exerts pressure it is the wood and not the concrete which cracks. The wood also, by its constant movement, tends to prevent the water icing over and preserves a breathing hole for fish. He keeps newts, tadpoles, daphnia and dragon flies in his pool and a few small lily pads that give shelter and shade, essential for fish who have no eyelids to keep out

Town Gardens to Live In

the glare. Once a pool like this has been going for a year it establishes a balance, but it must be allowed to go through the algae stage, after which it will clear. Be sure new plants are clean and are free of blanket-weed or duck-weed. Stones and rocks near the pool will make good hiding-places for many creatures. A more formal arrangement for a combined bird-splash and fish pool is illustrated on pp. 79–80.

## BIRDS

Birds can be encouraged to visit a garden by providing food; a nesting box may lead to a longer stay. Food can be put on a bird table, which may be a simple wooden platform on a four-foot high stake, or a specially designed piece of sculpture. Nestboxes can be fixed to a tree trunk or a wall, out of reach of cats and with some shade in summer. There should be no ledge beneath the entrance, as this might give a foothold to predators.

You can also grow food for your bird visitors and provide natural nesting places too, if you have room for a small tree, some large shrubs or a hedge. Seed-eating birds are specially attracted by all kinds of daisies, sunflowers, cosmos, asters of all kinds, antirrhinums and scabious. Insect-eating birds find plenty of food on the giant hogweed (pl. 123), but do not plant it when there are children too young to learn not to touch it, because it can cause an irritating rash on some people – stick to small birch trees or small willows, which also attract insects. Many birds enjoy berries; a list of the most popular is given on p. 134.

122. *A specially designed bird table*

123. *Giant hogweed* (Heracleum mantegazzianum) *in flower in the London garden in pl.* 84

Birds need water for drinking and bathing all the year round. Almost any large shallow container, such as an up-turned dustbin lid, can be used to make a bird-bath, sunk into the ground and placed away from bushes where cats might lurk. The inside of the bath should be rough, not slippery, and may have stones in the middle for the birds to perch on. You can also make a pool in an open part of the lawn, using a plastic material as described on pp. 166–7, but covering the edges with turf instead of stone. The pool should be shallow at one end and one to two feet deep at the other.

The Royal Society for the Protection of Birds will give advice on special food for certain species and on nesting boxes; they will also tell you which chemicals for garden use are harmful to birds.

Town Gardens to Live In

*Berrying plants that attract birds (prepared by the RSPB)*
Those most popular with the birds are listed first.
Elder (mainly *Sambucus nigra*); yew (*Taxus baccata*) – poisonous to humans; *Cotoneaster horizontalis* and *C. simonsii*; *Elaeagnus angustifolia* and *E. umbellata*; red and black chokeberries (*Aronia arbutifolia* and *A. melanocarpa*); barberry (*Berberis darwinii*); holly (mainly *Ilex aquifolium*); flowering currant (mainly *Ribes sanguineum*); honeysuckle (*Lonicera* species); hawthorn (mainly *Crataegus monogyna*); wayfaring tree (*Viburnum lantana*); blackberry (*Rubus fruticosus*); rowan (*Sorbus aucuparia*); firethorn (*Pyracantha coccinea*); crab apple (mainly *Malus pumila*); privet (mainly *Ligustrum vulgare*).

# BEES

There are about a thousand bee-keepers in London, where there are just as many flowers and less spraying than in the suburbs, hence more honey. In choosing a position for a hive, look for a dry, shady spot and avoid dark, damp corners. It must also be protected by the foliage of trees from excessive heat; otherwise the bees will swarm. Make sure that the flight path of the bees as they emerge from the hive does not cross a path used by people. Soothe anxious neigh-

124. *Beehives under a young willow in a north London garden. In the foreground, leeks grow among alpine strawberries*

The Naturalist

bours not only by gifts of honey, but by pointing out that their fruit trees will bear more fruit. This is especially so in a cold spring, when the bees do not have the time or inclination to roam far afield and so work the trees nearer home. Stand water near the hive, so shallow that small stones appear just above the water to serve as resting-places for the bees to stretch their wings on a hot day.

A National hive with a single wall will hold up to 50,000 bees. Sections are added vertically as the colony grows. It costs about £85 at 1977 prices to set up bee-keeping. The British Bee-keepers' Association will answer inquiries sent with a stamped-addressed envelope. The Ministry of Agriculture, Food and Fisheries publish a number of leaflets (e.g. no. 283, *Advice to Intending Beekeepers*).

*Plants that attract bees – a selection that provides for all seasons*

Asters; *Buddleia davidii*; *Caryopteris clandonensis*; *Chaenomeles speciosa* (ornamental quince); *Cornus mas* (Cornelian cherry); cotoneasters; flowering currant (*Ribes sanguineum*); golden rod (*Solidago*); *Rosa rubiginosa*; Salix caprea (goat willow); *Symphoricarpos orbiculatus* (coral berry).

## PLANTS

Naturalists are chiefly interested in flowers that grow in the wild, but protection and hospitality are also needed for certain groups of cultivated plants and vegetables; for example, the dianthus family, of which there were once many varieties. Today it is difficult to find the laced pinks and flakes that delighted our grandparents. They are rarely stocked by nurseries but can still be found in private gardens, whose owners may be persuaded to part with seeds or slips. The violet family is another casualty and so is the primrose, especially double varieties like the gorgeous Madame de Pompadour. To study a particular group of plants and build up a collection is a fascinating hobby and it is greatly to be hoped that current projects for compiling plant and vegetable registers will materialize. Meanwhile, the Hardy Plant Society (see p. 184) publishes a comprehensive list of herbaceous plants, including many rare varieties, with names and addresses of growers (*The Hardy Plant Directory*, available to non-members).

## 13 Roof Gardens

Wind, weight and water are the three chief problems in roof gardens. Winds and draughts are not only unpleasant for people: they can kill plants by drying up their leaves and rocking them if they are not firmly anchored. The weight of soil may, if excessive or badly distributed, damage the structure below. And plants must be watered every rainless day in summer.

It is seldom possible to eliminate wind completely; it can come from so many different directions, including down draught caused by surrounding buildings. Screens are the most effective answer, but they must be firmly secured. Wattle hurdles or wooden fencing give a sense of solidity; glass is lighter, and may be either transparent or opaque for greater privacy. Brick walls can be built up where the surroundings are ugly, leaving only one viewing space (pl. 125), glazed or open, or with an iron grille. There is, in any case, something to be said for limiting the view: total exposure to magnificent surroundings can be exhausting in the long run.

Unless your roof garden is on a very strong structure or over a supporting pillar, plant containers should be arranged round the sides. If in doubt, ask your landlord or a builder. It is generally safe to construct two or three permanent containers with brick or concrete retaining walls, capable of holding 12–18 in. of soil for larger plants. Smaller plants will make do in pots or window-boxes. These should be raised slightly above ground level, on bricks or small stones, to ensure good drainage. The permanent containers must also have drainage: roughly four inches of broken crocks or gravel at the bottom, covered by a layer of upside-down turves to prevent the water and soil running through and to act as an anchor for the plants. Weep-holes about 6 in. from the bottom will improve the drainage. Since there is no water to be drawn by capillary attraction from the earth beneath, as in normal conditions, the soil should contain plenty of humus to retain moisture: vermiculite, spent

*125. An open viewing space in a courtyard garden – an idea that could be adapted for a roof garden*

mushroom manure, bags of compost or rich loam mixed with bonemeal are all suitable. To prevent undue transpiration a mulch of peat, compost or leaf mould from the country should be spread over the surface after planting. An asbestos tile inserted vertically inside the front of the containers will prevent heat from reaching the roots of the plants, which tend to grow towards the edges of the container.

Watering can be made easier if the roof garden happens to be outside a bathroom or kitchen, even where there is no direct access. For a small sum (about £13 in 1977), a pipe from the domestic supply can be taken through the wall to the garden, with a tap on the outside and a stop-cock on the inside in case of frost. With direct access from the kitchen a hosepipe can be used. If there is room, it is a good idea to run water into a permanent outside container, where it can adjust to the same temperature as the soil; plants hot from the sun do not relish a flood of cold water. Water in the early morning or evening, not in the middle of the day.

The sun, too, can create problems. In great heat an asphalt floor can become so hot that large pots standing on it begin to sink in. Asbestos tiles (12 × 12 in.) laid on bitumen over felt make a better surface. They become warm but not hot and retain their heat, a point that appeals to sunbathers. They should be laid with a slight fall towards the nearest drainpipe. There should also be some overhead protection; a pergola, a light canopy or a beach umbrella. Glare can be minimized by avoiding too much white paint.

Town Gardens to Live In

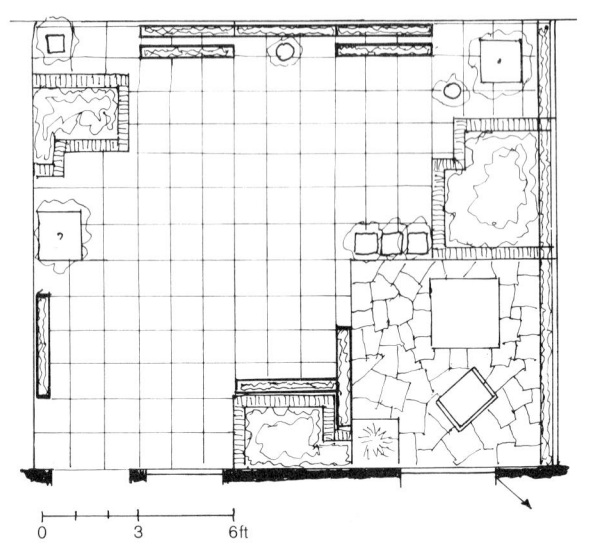

Fig. 24. *Plan of a north London roof garden. The use of a different paving material and slight change of level for the small sitting area has the effect of creating two separate spaces. Window-boxes along the outer wall are raised up one behind another to give a solid bank of flowers* (see pl. 126)

There is little possibility of pretence or illusion in a roof garden, but one owner has tried, by making a small raised platform for his sitting area, to give the impression that there are two separate compartments, between which he can move (fig. 24). The walls are planted out, in some places by a double row of window-boxes, the back row raised about nine inches on up-ended bricks, giving a solid bank of flowers from the parapet to the ground. Other boxes, mostly of wood, are hung at eye level and there are some large pots. The three permanent beds have brick retaining walls and contain a variety of climbers and shrubs. They act as a permanent green background, with slight variations of foliage, for bedding plants (geraniums and ox-eye daisies) in tones of pink and white, with drifts of lobelia, so much prettier than when it is dotted about. All the containers are stuffed with bulbs for the spring.

126. *A view of the roof garden in fig. 24, with an opaque glass screen*

127. *Planting in fibreglass containers on the roof garden that forms part of the German garden on pp. 35–6*

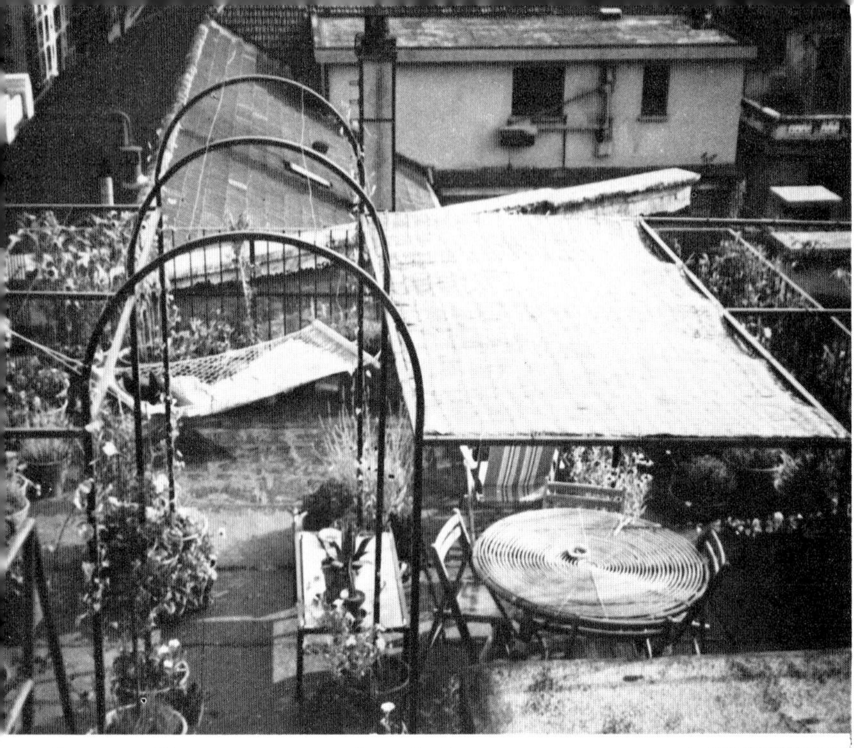

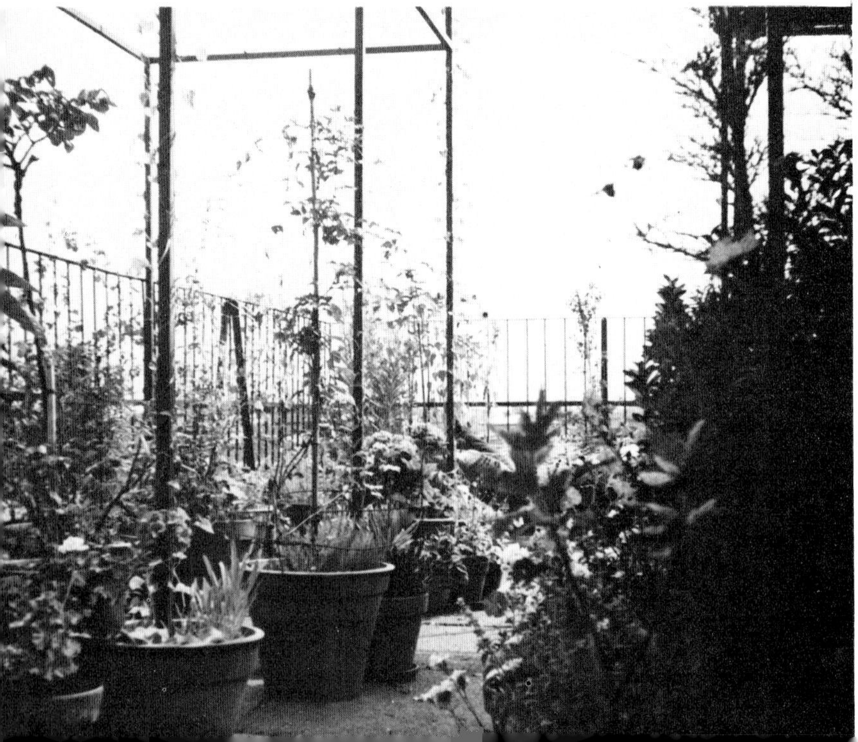

## Roof Gardens

128–9. *A roof garden in Milan. In summer, the garden is lived in from breakfast till bedtime – a good return for the money spent to make it habitable. A light metal structure covered with straw matting and Virginia creeper gives shade; the uprights are embedded in large flower-pots planted with climbers of all kinds. Matting woven between the railings round the edge keeps out wind, helped by more climbers (honeysuckle, clematis, Virginia creeper), whose green leaves counteract glare from the strong light. A few gaps are left, to give glimpses of the Milan churches. A system of water-proofed low-level lighting runs in a ring system round the terrace, so that there can be lights at any point, and two plugs for TV, record player, etc.*

*The roots of delicate plants are protected by sun-loving geraniums, mesembryanthemum, etc., planted in the same pot. Small pot plants cluster round the sides of big terracotta pots, to give more protection*

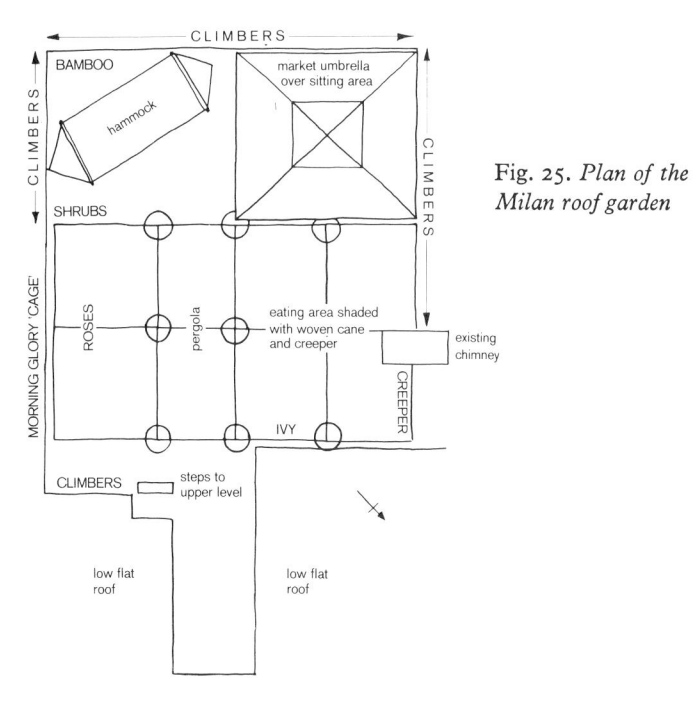

Fig. 25. *Plan of the Milan roof garden*

# Town Gardens to Live In

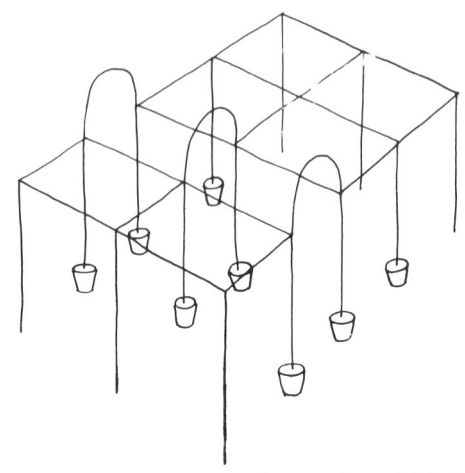

Fig. 26. *Sketch of the arrangement of the arches, which have their feet set in large flowerpots*

When making boxes avoid, if possible, using cheap deal or white wood. Even when treated inside against rot and given drainage holes they will soon disintegrate and the bottoms fall out. Better to spend a little more and make them of hard wood such as teak or oak. Wooden boxes filled with wet soil are very heavy and not easily moved. If the pots and containers are to be moved around to suit the season it is better to use fibreglass.

Vegetables can also be grown on a roof, larger plants in Gro-bags, small ones in pots. So can apples and pears that have been grown on dwarfing root-stocks, although they are not as prolific as in an orchard.

130. A balcony with a planting trough in the parapet

131. Tomatoes in Gro-bags masked by herbs in pots

132. A dwarf apple growing in a tub made of surplus wooden fencing with a polythene lining. It stands on bricks to give good drainage

## 14 Pots and Containers

All plants grown in pots and containers need ample water and drainage. Careful preparation of the pots is needed to meet these requirements. Drainage holes at the bottom of the container should be covered by a layer of clean broken pieces of pot, gravel or stone. Place on this a layer of dead leaves or, if available, a turf (grass side down) to retain moisture and prevent soil choking the crocks below. The life of all containers, especially wood, can be lengthened by fitting a lining of metal or polythene, but do not forget the drainage holes.

Moisture-loving plants such as ferns, hostas or hydrangeas will respond to a constant supply of moisture at their roots. This can be given by standing the pots in a non-porous tray or saucer filled with pebbles and water. The water-level should be adjusted so that it

133. *Pots in a London courtyard*

*134. Lilies and geraniums grouped on a small paved platform near the sitting area*

moistens only the lower crocks inside the pot, leaving the upper ones aerated. This gives plants the choice of damp or dry root conditions. Plants which prefer dry conditions should, on the contrary, be grown in containers standing clear of the ground, on bricks, slates or tiles, so that air can circulate beneath them and surplus water drain away. Most plant roots should be protected from excessive heat by placing a sheet of asbestos inside the container, on the sunny side.

Fill the pots with moist soil and, after planting, press firmly, leaving the soil surface about half to one inch below the rim to allow for watering. Remember that very little rain reaches the roots of potted plants and as they cannot draw water from the soil as other plants do, regular watering is essential. The risk of overwatering is prevented by the drainage at the base. Make sure that the soil is crumbly and fertile, or use one of the commercial composts suited to the plants you have chosen. In most cases it is advisable to give more water after planting.

Commercial composts, such as John Innes or Levington, are made in various mixtures, adapted to the needs of different plants. These are usually neutral in the chemical sense, that is, neither acid nor alkaline, to suit both lime-hating and lime-loving plants. For plants with special needs such as rhododendrons, which are lime-

*135. A shallow bowl bursting with sun-loving gazanias*

hating, or lavender, which prefers a limy soil, you can increase acidity by adding some peat, or add limestone chippings to make the mixture alkaline. Most of the lime-loving plants appreciate the sharper drainage provided by limestone grit.

Shrubs and perennials grown in pots will need occasional cutting back or pruning to keep them shapely. With care, hardy shrubs and some lilies and herbaceous plants can be kept undisturbed for several years in pots in the open if they are given occasional dressings of fresh compost on the surface and some balanced fertilizers in the water. Never exceed the suppliers' instructions, nor overfill the pot with fresh compost to the brim. Pour water on gradually, in several doses, to avoid the risk of dry cores developing in the containers if water overflows or soaks only down the sides of the container, and fork the surface of the soil lightly from time to time. Shrubs in pots may become root-bound after a few years and need re-potting.

Annual plants and most bulbs must be replaced, at suitable seasons, at least once a year. A continuous display of flowers can be obtained either by replanting (say with petunias to follow early bulbs) or by interplanting early and late flowering species together, for example hyacinths or polyanthus to flower in spring and tobacco plants (*Nicotiana*) to flower in summer and autumn. For really

*136. Pot plants in metal brackets on a wall*

long-flowering plants to be grown in pots on their own, try pot marigolds (*Calendula*) or petunias. Sweet peas grown from seed and trained up four or five canes joined together at the top to form a wigwam or pyramid will continue for quite a long time if you keep cutting the flowers. A very early display – short but gay – can be had by using the bulbous *Iris histriodes* Major or the Kaufmanniana tulip Heart's Delight. There will still be time to change these, after flowering, to petunias or some other plant. Ideally, fresh soil should be given at each repotting to ensure the best possible results, though this may not be strictly necessary. The really important thing is to ensure that the soil crumbles easily, is porous and evenly packed in round the roots, and that the drainage arrangements remain in good order.

Containers come in all shapes and sizes. Ordinary flowerpots, wooden tubs and fibreglass containers are easiest to obtain and are not expensive. For trees and very large shrubs with a big root system, concrete containers are one of the best solutions (pl. 138). Poking round junk shops may yield an old lead container or some discarded domestic object like an earthenware sink – the ideal way to grow alpines in a town garden. More expensively, one or two garden centres have pots from Italy and craft centres sell modern hand-thrown pots which add distinction to any garden. Amateur

137. Bergenia in a tub: good in shade as well as sun

138. Majorca oval concrete container by Mono Concrete, suitable for small trees or large shrubs

139. Hand-made stoneware pots
140. Stoneware boxes

## Pots and Containers

potters with access to a fairly large kiln could try their hand at simple shapes, such as those illustrated (pls. 139–42). But don't forget to make holes in the bottom, for drainage.

Plants make their maximum impact when the containers vary in size. A group made up of ageratum in a shallow bowl, ivy-leaved geraniums and blue-and-white striped petunias in slightly taller pots, with a flowering shrub (perhaps a white hydrangea) in a large pot to add solidity, will give pleasure from mid-June to September. For late spring you might have early single or double (April-flowering) tulips in the shallow bowl – they look well in shallow bowls as they have shorter stems than Darwin or cottage tulips – and wallflowers in the taller pots. Pots of geraniums and annuals should look as though they were bursting with flowers and foliage; the whole effect should be exuberant, so plant closer than you would in a flower-bed.

Few herbaceous perennials are happy in pots, but agapanthus, the African lily, is a good subject to grow in strong containers, since it flowers best when its fleshy roots are pot-bound and excessive growth of the strap-shaped green leaves is discouraged. Most varieties are hardy in the south and they all like a sunny, sheltered position. Flowers are encouraged by an annual dressing of sulphate of potash or woodash in the spring.

Scented-leaved geraniums (pelargoniums) are another of the joys of pot gardening. The flowers are insignificant for the most part, but brush your hand lightly against their leaves and faint waves of

141–2. *Terracotta pots*

## Town Gardens to Live In

lemon, orange or balsam will float out. Clorinda, with large rose-pink flowers, smells of cedar; the leaves of *P. crispum* Variegatum have cream variegations and smell of lemon. Most beautiful of all are the large downy leaves of peppermint-scented *P. tomentosum*. These geraniums need winter protection and should be brought into the house or into a greenhouse or similar shelter. Another tender plant with scented leaves is lemon-scented verbena (*Lippia citriodora*). Larger than the geraniums, its winter protection is more difficult to arrange.

Lilies are excellent in pots. Their beauty and fragrance are so lovely that it is worth the trouble to grow them well. Most prefer a lime-free soil, rich in leaf mould, peat or well-decayed manure with plenty of moisture and good drainage. *Lilium auratum* and its many hybrids and *Lilium speciosum* show themselves off to best advantage when planted singly, so that their elegant shape and huge flowers can be enjoyed. Many need protection in winter: pots plunged to the rim in a cool part of the garden and covered with an inch of leaf mould can remain there until the lilies are coming into flower, when they can be brought to their summer position in all their beauty. *Lilium regale*, however, is a very hardy lily that likes lime: it increases if left undisturbed in pots.

## Pots and Containers
## *MORE PLANTS SUITABLE FOR GROWING IN CONTAINERS*
*Evergreen shrubs for large containers*

|  | Height in feet | Colour of flower | Season | Remarks |
| --- | --- | --- | --- | --- |
| Azaleas (evergreen) | 2½–4 | all except yellow and blue | April–May | ½ shade but will stand full sun |
| Box, Silver (*Buxus sempervirens* Elegantissima) | 2½–4 |  |  | Full shade |
| Camellias |  |  |  |  |
| sasanqua group | 5–8 | white, pink, crimson | Dec.–March | Both groups need wall protection and should not receive early morning sun |
| japonica group | 5–8 | white, pink, crimson | Feb.–May | Will grow in ½ shade |
| *Choisya ternata* | 5–6 | white | May–June | Fragrant. Sun or shade |
| *Daphne odora* Aureomarginata | 2 | purple | Jan.–Feb. | Fragrant. Sun |
| *Fatsia japonica* | 8 | off-white | Oct. | Semi-shade |
| *Hebe anomala* | 3 | white | June–July | Full sun |
| *Hebe parvifolia* | 5 | pink | July–Aug. | Full sun |
| *Laurus nobilis* (bay) | 6–8 | yellow | April | Sun or shade |
| *Lavandula* (lavender) | 1½–3 | blue | July–Aug. | Sun |
| *Olearia hastii* | 4–5 | off-white | July–Aug. | Sun or shade |
| *Pieris formosa forrestii* | 4–5 | white | April | Red leaves when young. Shade |
| *Prunus laurocerasus* Zabeliana | 2½ | white | April | Sun or shade |
| Rhododendron (dwarf and slow-growing) | 1–10 | all | March–July | ½ shade or shade |
| Rosemary (*Rosmarinus*) | 3 | blue | April–May | Fragrant. Sun |
| Rue (*Ruta graveolens*) | 2 | yellow | August | Sun or ½ shade |
| Sage (*Salvia officinalis* and its variety, Purpurascens) | 2½ | blue | June | Sun |
| *Santolina chamaecyparissus* | 2 | yellow | July–Aug. | Sun or ½ shade |
| *Senecio greyi* | 2½ | yellow | June–July | Sun or shade |
| *Skimmia japonica* Foremanii | 3 | white | April–May | Shade |
| *Yucca filamentosa* | 3 | white | July–Aug. | Sun. Spiky foliage |

# Town Gardens to Live In

## Deciduous shrubs for large containers

|  | Height in feet | Colour of flower | Season | Remarks |
| --- | --- | --- | --- | --- |
| Azaleas (deciduous) | 4–6 | all except blue | May–June | ½ shade |
| *Berberis thunbergii* and *B.t. atropurpurea* | 4–5 | yellow | April–May | Sun or ½ shade |
| *Daphne mezereum* | 3–4 | white or purple | Feb.–March | Sun or shade |
| *Fuchsia magellanica* | 3–4 | crimson | July–Oct. | Sun or ½ shade |
| *F.m.* Gracilis | 2–3 | red and purple | June–Oct. | Sun or ½ shade |
| *F. m.* Riccartonii | 3–4 | red and purple | June–Oct. | Sun or ½ shade |
| *F. m.* Versicolor | 3–4 | red and purple | June–Oct. | Sun or ½ shade. Striped leaves |
| *Hydrangea macrophylla* (hortensias and lacecaps) | 3–4 | blue, pink, white | July–Sept. | Sun or ½ shade. Needs plenty of water |
| *Hypericum forrestii* | 3–4 | yellow | July–Sept. | Shade |

## Annuals and bedding for shallow bowls

| | | | | |
| --- | --- | --- | --- | --- |
| Ageratum | 6–12 | blue and purple | June–Sept. | Sun or shade |
| *Alyssum maritimum* | 6–8 | white | May–Sept. | Sun |
| *Begonia semperflorens* (fibrous-rooted) | 6–12 | white, pink, red | May–Oct. | Sun or shade |
| Gazania | 4–9 | orange and yellow | June–Sept. | Sun |
| Mesembryanthemum | 4 | crimson | June–Sept. | Sun |
| Petunia | 12 | all except yellow | June–Sept. | Sun or shade. Long flowering period |
| *Phlox drummondii* | 6–9 | white, red, pink | June–Aug. | |
| Polyanthus | 12 | all | March–June | Sun or shade |
| Viola (bedding and pansy) | 6–8 | most | March–Oct. | Sun or shade |

## Pots and Containers

### *Annuals and bedding for medium-sized containers*

|  | Height in inches | Colour of flower | Season | Remarks |
|---|---|---|---|---|
| Antirrhinum | 6–24 | all except blue | June–Sept. | Sun or shade |
| Arctotis (African daisy) | 12–18 | all except blue | June–Aug. | Sun |
| *Calendula* (pot marigold) | 18–24 | orange and yellow | May–Sept. | Sun |
| *Cheiranthus allionii* (Siberian wallflower) | 16 | yellow and orange | March–June | Sun or shade |
| *Cheiranthus cheiri* (wallflower) | 12–18 | all except blue | March–May | Sun or shade |
| Dahlia (Coltness and other dwarf hybrids) | 12–18 | all | July–Oct. | Sun or ½ shade |
| Heliotrope | 18–24 | blue and purple | June–Aug. | Sun |
| *Impatiens balsamina* (balsam) | 10–20 | white, pink, red | June–Aug. | Sun or shade |
| *Nicotiana* (tobacco) | 12–30 | white, red, pink, green | June–Sept. | Sun or ½ shade |

### *Perennials suitable for pots in shade, if kept moist*

|  |  |  |  |  |
|---|---|---|---|---|
| Bergenia | 12–18 | pink and crimson | March–May | Evergreen |
| *Dryopteris filix-mas* (male fern) | 24–36 |  |  |  |
| *Hosta sieboldiana* (syn. *glauca*) (plantain lily) | 24 | white/lilac | June–July |  |
| *Osmunda regalis* (royal fern) | 48–65 |  |  |  |
| *Phyllitis scolopendrium* (hart's tongue fern) | 18 |  |  | Evergreen |

### *Bulbs*

|  |  |  |  |  |
|---|---|---|---|---|
| *Amaryllis belladonna* | 24 | white and pink | Sept.–Oct. | Sun |
| Crinum | 30 | white and pink | July–Aug. | Sun |
| *Fritillaria imperialis* | 36 | yellow and orange | May | Sun or ½ shade |
| Hyacinth | 12–18 | all | April–May | Sun or shade |
| *Iris histrioides* Major | 8 | blue | February | Sun and sharp drainage |
| Lily | 24–60 | all except blue | March–Oct. | Sun or ½ shade |
| Tulip (early single or double) | 12–18 | all except blue | April | Sun or ½ shade |
| *Tulipa kaufmanniana* | 6–8 | cream, pink, orange, yellow, scarlet | March | Sun or ½ shade |

## 15 Front Gardens

The chief function of a front garden is to separate the house from the road and protect it from the noise and dust of traffic. It must also provide access, not only to the front door but to other parts of the house: to dustbins in a basement area, for example. It is decidedly not the place to grow your most precious plants, but flowers and foliage will give pleasure to passers-by as well as to yourself.

In a busy street, the traditional clipped privet hedge about five feet tall can cut out some of the noise and dust and give some degree of privacy. It also hides from the occupants of the house cars parked in the street outside and discourages dogs on the loose. A solid well-kept hedge adds to the architecture of the street. But it has disadvantages. It needs six or seven cuts in a summer, and the space it encloses is often overshadowed and airless. So rather than a discouraged patch of grass, cover it with rectangular paving and a few suitable plants in tubs or pots or growing in gaps in the paving. This is a last resort, for use where the problem of noise and dust is acute.

In quieter districts, where no hedge is needed, a ground covering of ivy or periwinkle with one or two larger evergreens strikes a

143. *See fig. 27*

Front Gardens

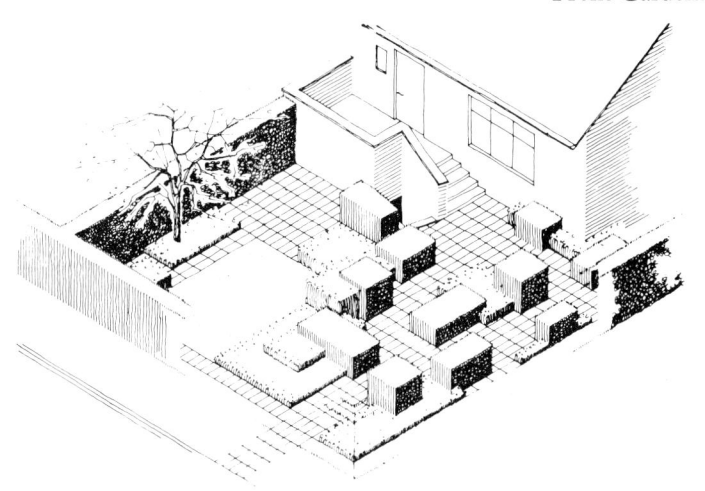

Fig. 27. *Bird's eye view of a Danish front garden with a pattern of blocks of privet and flower-beds (see pl. 143)*

refreshing note of green among bricks and mortar and can provide a dignified setting for a whole street if the residents can agree on a common policy.

A more creative use of privet has been devised for a front garden in Denmark (pl. 143). Blocks of small-leaved *Ligustrum vulgare* Sempervirens have been clipped into cubes and rectangles of varying heights to make a three-dimensional pattern, combined with geometrical beds of flowers with compact growth like *Aster amellus*, that carry the flower at the top of the stalk. For a permanent trouble-free arrangement *Hypericum calycinum* and grey-leaved cotton lavender (*Santolina chamaecyparissus*) could take the place of the flowers. Box or *Lonicera nitida* (a small-leaved evergreen shrubby honeysuckle) could be used instead of privet. The honeysuckle becomes leggy when allowed to grow tall but remains bushy when kept to a height of two feet or so.

Informal planting in a front garden has a relaxed and welcoming air. The plants used should be easily maintained shrubs: senecio, hellebores, euphorbias, viburnums and roses would be suitable for a sunny position. They should be protected from dogs and other

144. *A red Japanese maple* (Acer palmatum *Dissectum Atropurpureum*) *in a bed of variegated small periwinkle surrounded by* Cotoneaster salicifolius *Autumn Fire on two sides and yellow-flowered* Potentilla *Elisabeth on the third*

145. *Informal planting in a London front garden, protected by a thorny* Rosa paulii

146. *Window-boxes at eye-level beside a path*

147. *A basement area garden with planting of mimosa, fatsias and camellias*

148. *A front garden in Islington divided by steps down to the dustbins in the basement area*

149. *Shade planting beside a Chelsea house: ferns, hostas, bergenias, laurels and viburnums*

150. *The entrance courtyard of a house in Hatfield New Town*

## Town Gardens to Live In

encroachments by a large thorny rose along the front, planted sufficiently far back from the street to avoid tearing the clothes of passers-by – new growths should be tied back to the main stems from time to time. Window-boxes at eye-level beside a path also give a gay welcome and can provide colour nearly all the year (pl. 146).

Old houses in central areas have special problems. Often the front garden is just a basement area. Whitened walls give increased light for plants as well as people and show off to perfection the shadows of feathery shrubs like mimosa and the shapely leaves of fatsias (pl. 147).

Access to dustbins stored in a front area is another problem in some old houses. The path down to the area often cuts the front garden into two awkwardly shaped plots that are difficult to maintain. Planting in the garden in pl. 148 is permanent and needs little attention. Yet it is quite colourful, especially in winter: red berries of *Cotoneaster horizontalis*, blue-green leaves of rue, bronze epimediums and the lilac-pink and white hues of the leaves of *Euonymus fortunei radicans* Silver Queen. Green and white ivy (*Hedera canariensis* Variegata (syn. Gloire de Marengo)) climbs up the railings and screens the basement windows from passers-by. Other houses have a completely shaded path along one side of the house (pl. 149). Shade planting again comes to the rescue: ferns,

151. *Car-ports are a part of the street architecture of a housing estate at Milton Keynes New Town*

152. *New terrace housing in Camden Town. Each house has a ramp down to the garage on the right and a path leading off to the recessed house entrance on the left. The small gardens are protected from the street by shrubs and small trees in rectangular white containers*

variegated hostas, bergenias, viburnums, etc., planted in soil previously enriched by long-term fertilizers (see p. 102).

Another problem is the car which cannot be parked in the road. New housing estates may have car-ports which then become part of the street architecture. New terrace housing with built-in garages require other solutions, some of which are quite attractive, as in pl. 152. For older houses with space at the side a perspex-covered

153. Vitis coignetiae *trained over a light metal structure to make a shaded car-port*

## Town Gardens to Live In

car-port at one side is fairly unobtrusive but can become hot in summer. A large-leaved vine such as *Vitis coignetiae* trained over a light metal structure keeps the car cool and adds to the general appearance of the house (pl. 153).

Off-street parking can take up much of the front garden, leaving a patch too small for anything but paving. If you like your front garden to look green, you might consider using Monoslabs, made by Mono Concrete. These are pre-cast dark concrete slabs with an overall grid pattern made by gulleys deep enough (about 1 in.) to make pockets in which grass seed can grow (pl. 154). The slabs are about $1\frac{1}{2} \times 2$ ft. They need no joining and on most soils (*not* clay) the only foundation necessary for light vehicle parking is a one-inch layer of sharp sand spread on levelled ground. At 1977 prices an area $6 \times 14$ ft would cost about £44, plus £6.33 haulage. A cheaper solution would be to lay two wheel-tracks of Monoslabs, with grass between, but this is less satisfactory.

154. *A parking area of Monoslabs and grass*

## 16 Utilities

A beautiful garden can be spoiled by unglamorous objects like dustbins, washing, etc. Remember them when making your plan, and place them where they will do least harm. Steps can also be taken to make them relatively unobtrusive.

Dustbins are the most difficult to deal with. The two basic requirements are that they should be kept in shade as far as possible, for health reasons, and should be easy to get at. One solution is to keep them in low wooden cupboards with hinged doors, rather like a kitchen unit (pl. 155). The top of the cupboards can be used as a stand for a window-box or plants in small pots. Another possibility is to make a brick or concrete shelter. This may be covered with decorative tiles and used as a stand for pot-plants (pl. 156). A small hedge of privet, about four feet high, will make a good screen in a year or two. Better still, a trellis with ivy growing up it gives instant results and looks less like an after-thought. If the dustbins stand on a hard base, the ivy can be planted in a long container about a foot wide, like a window-box, into which the trellis itself is set. It would then look like the hedges used to create separate compartments in pl. 157.

155. *A wooden dustbin container with hinged doors*

156. *A tiled concrete dustbin shelter*

157. *Screens of ivy-covered trellis in long wooden boxes*

158. *The back entrance to a garden, with dustbins on the right, concealed in a cage of squared trellis. The cage has a hinged lid that lifts up to allow the bins to be filled, and a hinged front, secured by a bolt, that opens out when the bins are emptied. Ivy covers the cage, the arch and the gate itself, all from one plant*

Many people now have washing-machines and driers and Monday mornings are no longer quite so alive with flapping sheets and clothes. For those who prefer to dry their laundry out of doors, a small yard with a drying umbrella can be devised, either at the side of the house (where there is usually plenty of wind) or cut off from the end of a terrace by a fence through which air can pass (pl. 159).

159. *A small yard with a drying umbrella, separated from a sitting-out terrace by a ventilated fence*

Greenhouses can look out of place if they are dumped in a corner by themselves. Put next to the sitting area, they become an extension of the whole living space, rather like a Victorian conservatory, to be enjoyed by all the family. This may also solve the problem of what is to have first claim on the sunniest part of the garden.

A compost heap and a space for potting, etc., are part of every gardener's working equipment. In many gardens they can be tucked away behind a hedge at the end of the garden, but this is too great

160. *The greenhouse is part of the open-air living space*

161. *A sheltered potting area*

162. *Behind the wattle hurdles is the potting area. A similar box in the opposite corner contains the compost*

a sacrifice of space in a very small garden. The potting area might find a home in a corner near the house and be given overhead protection. Or it might be enclosed within a small box of wattle hurdles in one corner, with a similar box containing the compost in the opposite corner, leaving the full length of the garden visible in the centre.

Compost needs ventilation if it is to rot down properly, because the essential micro-organisms die if they are deprived of air or if the heap becomes waterlogged, although they do like a warm damp atmosphere. So it is no good piling up leaves, branches and other garden rubbish in a corner and hoping for the best. Containers of folding wire panels are available from hardware stores and are well suited to small gardens. You can also make a container, two or three feet square, of wooden slats, wire mesh or loose brick with ventilation holes. The heap should have a base of rubble for drainage and some protection from heavy rain. Use an activator, such as Adco or Garotta to speed the process of rotting down. In areas where bonfires are forbidden, rose clippings, etc., can be burnt in an incinerator with a lid.

# Appendix 1: Construction Notes

## BRICK-RETAINING WALLS*

Brick-retaining walls should be laid with cement mortar, except where plants will cover the walls – lime mortar is better for plants. Most mortar is one part cement to three parts sand. For gardens, a mix of 1:1:6 cement–lime–coarse sand is a good compromise.

It is inadvisable to attempt a height of more than 36 inches without professional help. The thickness at any one point must never be less than one-third of the height (e.g. the lowest level of a three-foot wall, allowing for brick dimensions of 9 in. × $4\frac{1}{2}$ in., would be $13\frac{1}{2}$ in. – see fig. 28). The foundation should be 4–6 in. concrete extending 3 in. each side of the wall. Be sure to leave a small hole for drainage at intervals: even at this height the build-up up of water might overturn the wall. The holes should be as low as possible as the water seeping out will stain the brickwork.

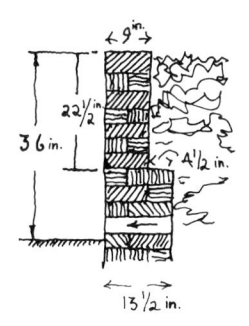

Fig. 28. *Diagram of a section of 36 in. high retaining wall showing weep hole and set back to ensure that the wall thickness is never less than one third of the height*

* The above notes are intended for general guidance. For detailed construction techniques, consult a good manual such as the *Reader's Digest Complete Do-it-yourself Manual*. Three leaflets on simple brick structures are available from the Brick Development Association, 19 Grafton Street, London W1X 3LE.

Town Gardens to Live In

The way in which the bricks are arranged, i.e. the bonding, can vary greatly. On no account should one mortar joint come above another; there must always be an overlap by a half or a third. The top course should be $4\frac{1}{2}$ in. brick on edge. If you would like to have plants growing out of the wall you could miss out a header, or half a brick, in one or two places.

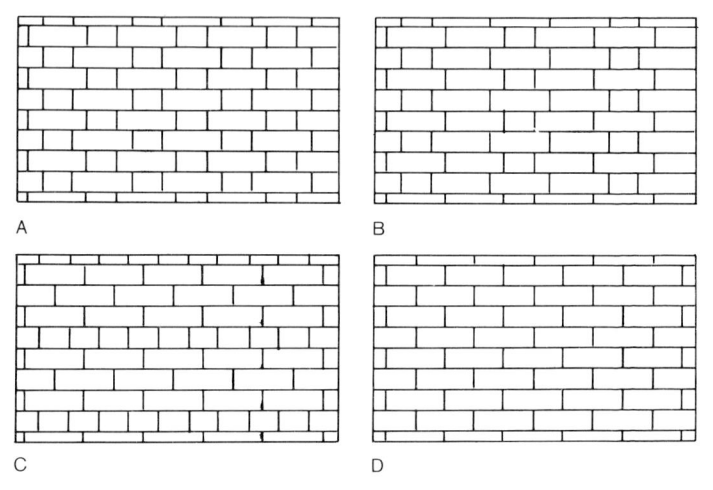

Fig. 29. *Brick bonds:* (a) *Flemish bond – alternating and staggered headers and stretchers. Easy to lay and strong;* (b) *Flemish garden-wall bond – three stretchers in a row, alternating with one header. More economic than Flemish bond;* (c) *English garden-wall bond, economic and easy to lay;* (d) *stretcher bond – the most economic, but it could be out of scale in a small garden*

## HOW TO MAKE AN INFORMAL POOL, USING A PLASTIC LINER

(1) Excavate the hole to the required shape and size, removing sharp stones, etc., and lining the surface with a layer of damp soft sand.

(2) Stretch the plastic liner over the hole with an all-round overlap and place heavy stones or bricks round the outer edge of the liner (the length of the liner should be not less than the overall

Appendix 1: Construction Notes

length of the pool plus twice the maximum depth, the width should be the overall width of the pool plus twice the maximum depth).

(3) Run water slowly on to the liner, which will gradually sink into the hole and be moulded to the sides by the water's weight.

(4) When the pool is full, trim off surplus liner, leaving about nine inches all round, and cover with heavy stones laid at the edge of the pool to hold the plastic in position.

## CONCRETE

The following is extracted from *Concrete in Garden-making*, a well-illustrated booklet obtainable free of charge from the Publications Sales Unit of the Cement and Concrete Association, Wexham Springs, Slough SL3 6PL:

### Mixes

For most concrete work in the garden one of three basic mixes will do the job. Mix A is a general purpose mix. Mix B should be used where strength or resistance to wear is important. Mix C is suitable for very thin sections or for bedding mortars.

Mix A: 1 part cement, $2\frac{1}{2}$ parts sand, 4 parts coarse aggregate – by volume. Suitable for footings, garage floors, drives and thick walls.

Mix B: 1 part cement, 2 parts sand, 3 parts coarse aggregate – by volume. Suitable for paths, pools, steps, garden frames, pots, edging and thin sections.

Mix C: 1 part cement and 3 parts sand – by volume.

Too much water should not be used as this will weaken the concrete and cause shrinking when it hardens; on the other hand the mix must be workable enough to be put into the moulds and compacted without leaving air-holes or 'honeycombing'.

### Mixing concrete

#### Hand-mixed concrete

Where the quantities of concrete involved are small, it is perfectly simple to mix the material you require yourself.

167

Town Gardens to Live In

The concrete should be mixed on a clean, hard surface or a platform of boards. It is important to use clean sand, clean coarse aggregate and clean water. Clean materials and working conditions are particularly important when using a coloured cement, which must also be kept away from cements of other colours.

All ingredients, including the water, should be carefully measured in order to obtain uniform concrete and to avoid waste; for small jobs buckets are convenient for this purpose, provided they are all the same size. Use one bucket for cement only; a second bucket can be used for the sand, coarse aggregate and the mixing water. Using a 1:2:3 mix (mix B), take 1 bucket of cement, 2 of sand, 3 of gravel or broken stone, and about $\frac{3}{4}$ of a bucket of water.

Make sure you have the correct amount of water, as the shape of a bucket makes it difficult to estimate quantities by eye. Do not use too much water: the drier the mix, provided it is workable, the better the concrete.

First form a flat circular layer with the measured quantity of coarse aggregate, then add the measured quantity of sand. Add the cement, mainly in the centre, and mix by turning twice. Form a crater and pour in half to two-thirds of the total water. Then sprinkle the dry material from the outside into the centre and turn it all over, adding more water from a watering can fitted with a fine rose. Knead the heap with the flat of a shovel to speed the mixing, and continue turning until the mix is uniform. It is most important to ensure that the materials are thoroughly mixed after adding the water.

*Dry-mixed concrete*

Mixing concrete by hand can be simplified by using 'dry-mix' concretes. These are obtainable in one-hundredweight bags from builders' merchants, and are very useful where only small quantities of concrete are involved. The mix required should be specified when ordering. The contents of the bag should be well turned over on emptying out; all the stones will be at the bottom in mixes containing coarse aggregate. The water should then be added and mixing completed as described for hand-mixing.*

* Concrete can also be bought ready-mixed if a large area is to be covered. S. J.

Appendix 1: Construction Notes

*Placing concrete*

However you choose to mix or obtain your concrete it should be placed within one hour. It must then be well-compacted. It must also be protected from the drying action of sun and wind and be kept damp for about three days. The easiest way of doing this is to cover it with a sheet of polythene fixed all round and weighed down with a thin scatter of sand.

Remember to wash down the surface or boards on which the concrete has been mixed as soon as concreting has been completed, taking care to see that the cement or sand does not get into the house or yard drains. A dry sweep of the area before washing will reduce the amount being washed away to a very small quantity. Also wash your tools.

Do not concrete in really cold weather, though a slight night frost will do no harm if the concrete is well covered.

*Ready-made paving slabs and how to lay them*

Precast slabs can be obtained from garden centres and suppliers throughout the country or from concrete product makers. If desired, areas of cobbled finish can be introduced among the slabs. The range of possibilities is immense and can usefully be investigated before planning the work.

First of all prepare the site by removing the top soil and seeing that the ground is even and firm; where the ground is inclined to be soft, hardcore, well rolled in and finished with fine material, ensures a satisfactory base. String lines should be set along either side of the path or area to keep the outside edges straight. Always check for level before laying.

Next, bed the slabs, one at a time, on mortar mix C, which should be spread over the ground to a thickness of about 1 in. The joints between the slabs should be preferably about $\frac{1}{2}$-in. wide; small pieces of wood can be inserted temporarily between the slabs while they are being placed to help keep the spacing regular. Each slab should be lightly tapped into position until any tendency to rock is eliminated. The level of each slab must be checked to see that it is correct before proceeding with bedding the next slab.

Slabs can also be bedded on a $1\frac{1}{2}$–2 in. bed of sand in the same way, or on raked earth, but there will be some danger of settlement or movement.

The joints of the slabs bedded on mortar should be filled with mix C; a minimum of mixing water should be added to avoid producing a mortar that is wet and sloppy. Pack each joint with mortar and ram it well in. Then rub it with a piece of wood, so that the mortar is slightly lower than the surface of the slabs. Any mortar that is dropped on to the slabs should be sponged off as each joint is completed.

Alternatively, the joints can be filled with sand, or with dry-mix mortar placed $\frac{1}{4}$ in. below the surface and watered in. The slabs can also be laid close-jointed.

## *How to make an in situ concrete path*

Although this involves more work it is more economical to lay a concrete path *in situ* (i.e. the freshly-mixed concrete placed direct on the site). For this type of path the surface can be left smooth, or lightly brushed to give an interesting texture, or can be brushed more strongly to expose the aggregate.

Mix B should be used for an *in situ* path. A nominal thickness of three inches of concrete is recommended.

Remove the surface material down to at least three inches below the proposed finished level of the path. Fill any soft areas with hard core or broken stone and roll the whole length of the path to compact it. Thorough compaction of the bed is most important. Again, check for level before starting the path. Then lay strong pieces of wood, of a depth equal to the thickness of the concrete required, to act as forms (i.e. the frame of mould in which the concrete is cast) along each side of the path. A guiding string is used to obtain a straight line for setting the forms. Then pegs should be driven in against the outside of the forms to keep them in line when the concrete is being placed against them.

The path should be given a crossfall, especially away from the house wall, to allow water to drain away. The amount of crossfall necessary depends on the width of the path – say, 1 inch in 6 feet – and it is obtained by setting one form lower than the other. The

## Appendix 1: Construction Notes

forms can be checked for level by placing a wood block of the thickness of the crossfall on the lower form, and checking with a spirit level on a straight edge laid across the forms. The pegs should then be nailed to the forms.

Concreting can either be done continuously or by alternate bays. In either case the path should be laid in bays about eight feet long.*
Because concrete expands and contracts with changes of temperature it is necessary to break up the concreting into strips. If concreting is continuous from bay to bay, thin softwood laths, left permanently in place, can be used for this purpose. If the concrete is placed in alternate bays, temporary boards of stouter section are used, and removed when the concrete has hardened, leaving simple butt joints between the bays. The cross joints which are formed by both methods are necessary to prevent the risk of subsequent cracking.

If the ground is dry, damp the surface before placing the concrete. Mix enough concrete to complete one bay and lay it as soon as possible, and within an hour of mixing. Spread the concrete with a shovel, work it well into place and rake it down to a height of about $\frac{1}{4}$ in. above the top of the side forms.

Compact the concrete with a punner or by working a length of board, slightly wider than the path, over the surface, first with a chopping motion and then with a sawing motion, resting this wooden board on the side forms. A slightly rippled surface can be produced in this way. A smoother surface can be obtained, if desired, by finishing it with a wooden float. In continuous construction the concrete either side of the joint must also be fully compacted.

At the end of a day's work a stop end should be fixed across the path and concreting completed up to it, to make a vertical joint. When concreting continues a simple butt joint should be formed.

Do not forget to protect the freshly placed concrete from the sun, wind and rain – this is most important. As soon as the concrete has set sufficiently, cover it with polythene or with damp sacks which should be kept moist for about three days.

* Precast paving-slabs can be simulated by reducing the size of the bays and simulating a joint. S.J.

Town Gardens to Live In

If a brushed finish is required, the surface should be brushed with a soft broom to remove the surplus mortar about an hour after the concrete has been placed. If the aggregate is to be exposed the surface should be brushed again when the concrete has hardened to such an extent that the stones cannot be dislodged. The surface should then be sprayed with water, leaving the stones slightly 'proud' of the surface. Do not, however, apply this technique with coloured cements in cold, damp weather.

*Cobbled finish*

This can be obtained by bedding large stones or shingle about three inches or more in size in mortar on a concrete base. First lay concrete mix A at least three inches thick to form the base. Then spread a layer of mix C over the base, and place each stone by hand, so that just over half of its depth is bedded. Only small quantities of mix C should be made up at a time, as the rate it is used will depend on the rate of placing the stones. The usual procedure is to lay a stiff concrete base and then place the mortar topping within about one hour of laying the base. This ensures a good bond between the layer of stones and the base. Any mortar sticking to the top surface of the stones can be removed by washing and brushing

163. *Placing cobblestones in mortar on a concrete base*

Appendix 1: Construction Notes

about three hours after placing. A mixture of cobble stones and paving slabs makes possible a wide range of colour, pattern and texture combinations.

*How to build a raised bed using small walling units*

A proprietary miniature retaining wall unit, which is structurally self-sufficient, can be used to provide an easy-to-build raised bed. These precast units are three feet long by one or two feet high. They are aggregate-faced; right-angle external corners are provided by using mitre-end units.

These wall units are suitable for laying on most ground surfaces, providing adequate drainage exists or is specially provided. The ground should be prepared by levelling and consolidating to form a firm base. If ground conditions are unsuitable, a bed of lean mix concrete (say 1 of cement:8 of coarse aggregate) three inches thick can be laid to provide a firm base. The units should be bedded on a layer of mortar (mix C) not exceeding $\frac{3}{4}$ in.

Determine the line of each wall of the raised bed by using a taut string line. Place the units along this line on the mortar bed allowing a $\frac{3}{8}$-in. joint between each unit. Check for level both horizontally

164. *Container made with concrete slabs*

and vertically, using a spirit level and straight edge. When making a corner, check that the units are at right angles.

When all the units have been laid the back of each joint should be sealed with an adhesive tape* to prevent contamination of the unit face.

To prevent water weeping at the joints it is advisable to place a membrane of plastic sheeting at the back of the joints before the earth back fill is placed, which can be done immediately.

Finally, the joints can be sealed with mortar, if required. On completion, a wash down with clean water and a hard bristle brush will remove any dirt from the surface.

## *How to build a raised bed using pre-cast slabs*

A raised bed can also be made by the same method, but using concrete slabs. Polythene sheet should be placed over the joints to avoid moisture seepage and the bottom 6 in. of the bed should be filled with rubble for drainage. Further details can be obtained from the Disabled Living Foundation (see p. 184).

Obviously, this type of raised bed made with precast concrete slabs can have many attractions for the fully active as well as the disabled gardener.

## *How to make a small formal pool*

Pools more than about ten feet long or more than two feet deep may require heavier construction than that indicated here.

The pool can be painted, if required, using cement-based paints. The smooth surface of the paint will help to reduce the possibility of algae growth on the walls. The formal pool illustrated here (pls. 165, 166 and 167, and fig. 30) is six feet square and six inches deep. The dimensions of a pool of this type will, however, be influenced by whether precast paving slabs are used for the surrounds. If so, the size of the pool must be calculated in relation to the layout of the slabs.

The ground should be excavated to allow for the depth of the pool, plus a four-inch concrete base and six-inch thick walls. The level should be obtained with pegs and spirit level.

---

* Waterproof tape available from builders' merchants. S.J.

165. *Checking the level of the excavation for a small formal pool, using straight edge and spirit level*

166. *Placing and compacting the concrete for the walls of the pool. Note the timber formwork*

167. *Taking out the formwork*

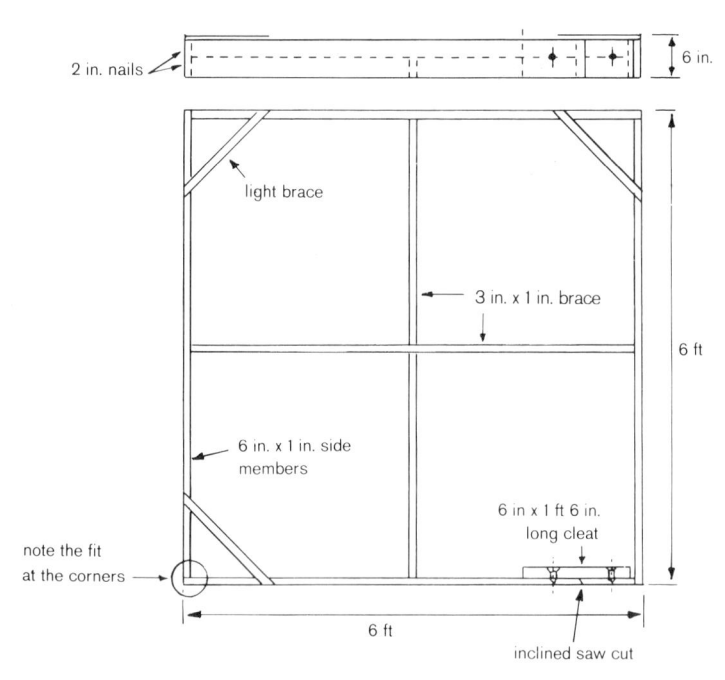

Fig. 30. *Formwork for pool, showing cleat*

## Appendix 1: Construction Notes

Mix B should be used for the concrete. The floor of the pool is concreted first and the surface tamped with a length of timber. When the concrete is just starting to harden – in normal weather about three hours after placing – the outer edge on which the walls will rest should be roughened by brushing or by raking the surface to provide a good key for the concrete of the walls. This treatment of the joint between the floors and walls is very important to ensure watertightness. If the pool is small and shallow and has sloping sides the floor and wall may sometimes be cast in one operation with advantage.

The formwork for the sides of the pool illustrated consists of one-inch thick timber, made up to the inner dimensions and depth of the pool, and braced by cross-pieces and corner-pieces. When the floor slab is at least one day old, place this formwork on the concrete floor. Check its position carefully, and thoroughly clean the joint surface round the outside. The surfaces of the formwork in contact with the concrete should be given a coat of oil or limewash before the concrete is placed, in order to prevent it from sticking to the concrete.

When placing and compacting the concrete for the sides take care not to move the formwork. To ensure thorough compaction of the concrete, tap the formwork with a hammer all round on its inner face.

The pool should be covered with polythene for twenty-four hours after placing, to cure the concrete.

The formwork can be removed within two or three days of placing the concrete. It can either be cut out piecemeal, or an inclined cut can be made on one side and covered with a cleat, when making up the formwork (fig. 30). To remove the formwork, unscrew the cleat and ease out at the cut.

It is advisable to fill the pool with water as soon as the formwork is stripped; this will help curing. During the first few days it is usual to find a noticeable drop in the water level as a certain amount of water is absorbed by the concrete.

The surround to the pool can be laid with precast slabs bedded in mix C using builders' sand. If the slabs project slightly over the edge of the pool they will hide any slight irregularities in the concrete. The floor of the pool can be tiled, if desired.

## *How to make a small informal pool*

A free-shaped concrete pool, or series of pools, can make a delightful feature in an informal garden. The method of making described here is suitable for a pool of up to ten feet maximum dimension.

First decide on the size and shape of the pool required, and make the excavation, trimming the sides to a gentle slope without disturbing the ground. Damp the soil with water to prevent absorption of water in the concrete. Next spread mix B with a trowel to a nominal three-inch thickness and finish it with a steel float and a ball of hessian to remove trowel marks, if desired. Cover with wet sacking or polythene to cure. If the pool is filled with water twenty-four hours after concreting, this will help the concrete to harden.

## *Maintenance of concrete pools*

### *Seasoning*

When a new pool is first filled with water it has to be seasoned before any fish or plant life can be introduced into it, otherwise the chemicals in the cement may harm them. This seasoning period takes approximately a month, and during this time the pool should be emptied and refilled two or three times. Each time the pool is emptied the sides and bottom should be scrubbed vigorously. Even at the end of the month it is advisable as a test to introduce a few small minnows or tadpoles into the water before stocking the pool with more valuable fish.

The seasoning period can be reduced by treating the sides with silicate of soda (waterglass) or proprietary products which are obtainable for this purpose.

### *Algae growth*

At times, certain forms of algae (microscopic plants) may develop in the pool and cause the water to become green and opaque.

Blanket weed, which is formed by algae, often proves troublesome, and if an excessive growth does appear in the pool, the fish and molluscs should be removed and the pool sterilized with

Appendix 1: Construction Notes

permanganate of potash. This can be done by putting the crystals in a muslin bag and swirling it in the water until the water is changed to a rich purple colour. After one day the pool should be emptied and filled with fresh water, taking care to remove as much of the solution as possible.

## IMPERIAL AND METRIC MEASURES

### Length

| Imperial | Metric |
| --- | --- |
| 1 inch | = 2·54 cm |
| 1 ft | = 30·48 cm |
| 1 yd | = 91·44 cm |

| Metric | Imperial |
| --- | --- |
| 1 cm | = 0·39 inch |
| 1 metre | = 3·28 ft |

### Area

| Imperial | Metric |
| --- | --- |
| 1 sq inch | = 6·45 cm$^2$ |
| 1 sq ft | = 0·09 m$^2$ |
| 1 sq yd | = 0·84 m$^2$ |

| Metric | Imperial |
| --- | --- |
| 1 cm$^2$ | = 0·16 sq inch |
| 1 m$^2$ | = 1·20 sq yd |

### Weight

| Imperial | Metric |
| --- | --- |
| 1 lb | = 454 g |
| 1 stone = 14 lb | = 6·35 kg |
| 1 cwt = 8 stone | = 50·80 kg |
| 1 ton = 20 cwt | = 1·02 tonnes |

| Metric | Imperial |
| --- | --- |
| 1 kg = 1000 g | = 2 lb 3 oz |
| 1 tonne = 1000 kg | = 0·98 ton |

# *Appendix 2: Finding Out*

This book does not attempt to give detailed information on how to grow plants because there are a number of excellent books on specialist subjects which are available from most public libraries. The catalogues of some of the larger nurseries also give valuable advice, with helpful lists of plants for different soils and situations. The selection of these and other useful sources given here is based on personal knowledge and is not intended to be comprehensive.

## BOOKS

*General*

> Boddy, F., *Foliage Plants*, David & Charles, 1973.
> Gemmell, Alan, *The Penguin Book of Basic Gardening*, Penguin Books, 1975.
> Hammett, K. R. W., *Plant Training, Pruning and Tree Surgery*, David & Charles, 1973.
> Hay, Roy, *The Modern Gardener*, Pearson, 1960.
> Hellyer, A. G. L., *Practical Gardening for Amateurs*, Collingridge, 1967.
> Pasley, A. du Gard, *Summer Flowers*, Allen Lane, 1977.
> *Reader's Digest Encyclopaedia of Garden Plants and Flowers*, Reader's Digest Association, 1971.
> Thomas, G. S., *Colour in the Winter Garden*, Dent, 1967.

*Bulbs*

> Doerflinger, Frederic, *The Bulb Book*, David & Charles, 1973.
> de Graaff, J., and Hyams, E., *Lilies*, Nelson, 1967.

*Ferns*

> Grounds, R., *Ferns*, Dent, 1974.

Appendix 2: Finding Out

*Ground cover*
>Boddy, F., *Ground Cover and Other Ways to Weed-free Gardens*, David & Charles, 1974.
>Fish, M., *Ground Cover Plants*, Collingridge, 1965.
>Thomas, G. S., *Plants for Ground Cover*, Dent, 1970.

*Perennials*
>Thomas, G. S., *Perennial Garden Plants*, Dent, 1976.

*Roses*
>Thomas, G. S., *The Old Shrub Roses*, Dent, 1961.
>Thomas, G. S., *Climbing Roses Old and New*, Dent, 1965.
>Thomas, G. S., *Shrub Roses of Today*, Dent, 1974.

*Trees*
>Grounds, R., *Trees for Smaller Gardens*, Dent, 1974.
>Huxley, A., *Evergreen Garden Trees and Shrubs*, Blandford Press, 1972.

*Vegetables and fruit*
>Royal Horticultural Society, *The Vegetable Garden Displayed*; *The Fruit Garden Displayed*.
>Seddon, G., *Your Kitchen Garden*, Mitchell Beazley, 1975.
>Simons, A. J., *The New Vegetable Grower's Handbook*, Penguin Books, 1975.

*Water gardens*
>Beedell, S., *Water in the Garden*, David & Charles, 1973.
>Perry, Frances, *The Garden Pool*, David & Charles, 1971.

*Window-boxes*
>Field, Xenia, *Window Box Gardening*, Blandford Press, 1974.

## CATALOGUES

Prices are correct at the time of going to press.

Hillier & Sons, Winchester, Hants., *Manual of Trees and Shrubs*. Describes 8,000 trees, shrubs, climbers, conifers and bamboos. General indications of plant heights; cultural notes; useful lists of plants for different situations. Price £3.20 incl. postage. *Hardy Perennial and Alpine Plants*, including hardy ferns and ornamental grasses. Gives heights and cultural hints. Price 50p incl. postage. *Roses and Fruit*. Price 30p incl. postage.

W. E. Th. Ingwersen, Birch Farm Nursery, Gravetye, East Grinstead, Sussex. Full cultural notes and descriptions of alpine and rock garden plants. Price 25p incl. postage.

Jackmans of Woking, Jackmans Nurseries, Woking, Surrey. *Planters Handbook* gives cultural notes on general nursery stock, including height and spread, habit, colour and flowering period. Price 25p.

Notcutt Nurseries Ltd, Woodbridge, Suffolk. Cultural notes on general nursery stock including height and habit. Price 50p.

John Scott & Co., The Royal Nurseries, Merriott, Somerset. Good fruit and rose sections. Cultural notes on general stock, including height and habit. Price 59p incl. postage.

Sunningdale Nurseries Ltd, Windlesham, Surrey. Good rose and rhododendron sections. Cultural notes on general nursery stock, including height. Price 40p incl. postage.

### *Specialist nurseries*

Alpines: C. G. Hollett, Greenbank Nursery, Sedbergh, Yorks.
Ferns: Reginald Kaye Ltd, Waithman Nurseries, Silverdale, Cornforth, Lancs; R. Hill, The Nurseries, Appleton, Abingdon, Berks.
Fruit: Blackmoor Nurseries, Blackmoor, Liss, Hants.
Geraniums: Greybridge Geraniums, Fibrex Nurseries, Harvey Road, Evesham, Worcs.
Roses: Blaby Rose Gardens, Lutterworth Road, Blaby, Leicester; Cant's of Colchester, Colchester, Essex;

Appendix 2: Finding Out

Friar's Nurseries, Knutsford, Cheshire; Gregory's Roses, Nottingham; John Mattock, Headington, Oxford; Edwin Murrell, Portland Nurseries, Otely Road, Shrewsbury; R. V. Rogers (The Nurseries Ltd), Pickering, Yorks.

Water plants: Highlands Water Gardens, Solesbridge Lane, Chorleywood, Herts; Garden Pools, Old Milverton Road, Milverton, Leamington Spa; Reginald Kaye Ltd (see under Ferns); Perry's Hardy Plant Farm, Enfield, Middlesex; Stapely Water Gardens, Stapely, Nantwich, Cheshire.

Seeds: Thompson & Morgan, London Road, Ipswich, Suffolk, have an enormous range of vegetable and flower seeds. W. W. Johnson, Boston, Lincs., specialize in grass seed. Carter's and Sutton's seeds are widely sold in hardware shops as well as garden centres.

## *SOCIETIES, ETC.*

The Institute of Landscape Architects, 12 Carlton House Terrace, London SW1Y 5AH, will supply names of professional landscape architects willing to give advice on layout, design and planting.

The Royal Horticultural Society, Vincent Square, London SW1, offers a number of services to members in return for a minimum subscription of £7.50. In addition to free admission to all the Society's shows and meetings and to their garden at Wisley, Surrey, these services include: free use of the library at Vincent Square; a free copy of the Society's monthly journal, *The Garden*; advice on horticultural problems, including the identification of plants and control of pests and diseases; soil and manure analyses and inspection of members' gardens by the Society's Adviser (a fee is charged for these services).

The Society also publishes a series of Wisley Handbooks giving practical information on a wide range of subjects; prices are 60–70p.

Town Gardens to Live In

The Royal National Rose Society, the National Chrysanthemum Society and the National Dahlia Society hold shows at the RHS Hall in Vincent Square, and there are a number of smaller societies concerned with the cultivation of a particular plant.

The Disabled Living Foundation, 346 Kensington High Street, London W14, gives advice on gardening for the disabled.

The Royal Society for the Protection of Birds, The Lodge, Sandy, Bedfordshire.

The British Beekeepers' Association, 55 Chipstead Lane, Sevenoaks, Kent TN13 2AJ.

The Hardy Plant Society (Hon. Sec.: Miss B. White, 10 St Barnabas Road, Emmer Green, Caversham, Reading RG4 8RA) publish *The Hardy Plant Directory*, which can be obtained from R. A. Grout, Colt House, Thurgarton, Nottingham (price £1·50 + 15p postage to non-members).

## *MATERIALS*

Concrete: *Concrete round the House* and *Concrete in Garden-making* can be obtained free of charge from the Publications Sales Unit, Cement and Concrete Association, Wexham Springs, Slough SL3 6PL.

Hand-made pots: The Craft Advisory Committee, 12 Waterloo Place, Lower Regent Street, London SW1, has a register of potters in all parts of the country.

Metal arches (p. 54): Frank Williams, The Old Post Office, Burford, Oxfordshire; Garden Furniture, High Street, Burford, Oxfordshire; Neale's Nurseries, Heathfield Road, London SW18.

Riviera fencing (p. 111): Gerald Gilmer Ltd, Southdown Works, South Street, Lewes, Sussex BN7 2BS.

Tiles (p. 80): Pilkington & Carter, P.O. Box 4, Clifton Junction, Manchester M27 2LD.

# *Index*

Page numbers of illustrations are in **heavy** type

acacia, see Robinia
*Acacia dealbata*, 99, 100
acanthus, 30, 32, 96
*Acer griseum*, 98
  *grosseri*, 98
  *palmatum* Atropurpureum, 32
  *p.* Dissectum Atropurpureum, 32, **156**
*Achillea* Moonshine, 30
aconite, winter, 100
aconitum, 32, 96
African daisy, 153
agapanthus, 149, **125**
ageratum, 149, 152
*Ailanthus altissima*, 51
*Ajuga reptans* Variegata, 99
*Akebia quinata*, 73
alder buckthorn, 131
*Allium cepa aggregatum*, 124
*Alyssum maritimum*, 32, 111, 152
  *benthami*, 131
*Amaryllis belladonna*, 153
*Amelanchier canadensis*, 43–5
anemone, 96
  Japanese, 32, 96
*Anemone hepatica*, 100
annuals, 32, 56, 146, 149
Antirrhinum, 32, 132, 153
apple, 26, 126–7, 142, **143**
  arches, 54
aquatic plants, 88–9
aquilegia, 30, 96
arbutus, 39, **41**
arches, 54
arctotis, 153
aronia, 134
*Artemisia ludoviciana*, 32
artichoke, globe, 122–3
*Aruncus dioicus*, 32

arundinaria, 52, 91
*Arundinaria murielae*, 31, 93, 103, **102**
  *nitida*, 31
asparagus, 122
*Asperula odorata*, 39, 96
aster, 132, 135, 155
astilbe, 32, 96
astrantia, 96
azalea, 15, 32, 96, 103, 151, 152

balsam, 153
bamboo, 31, 52, 91, 93, 103, 119, **102**
  screen, **75**
barbecue, 115, **114**
bay, 48, 96, 128, 151
beans, 122, 124
bedding plants, 31, 32, 56, 138
beds, raised, 95, 104, 136–8, 165, 173–4, **105**, **106**
beech, 70–71, 106
bees, 134–5
begonia, 32, 152
berberis, 96, 106
*Berberis darwinii*, 121, 134
  *thunbergii*, 152
  *t.* Atropurpureum, 32, 152
bergamot, 32, 96
bergenia, 96, 153, 159, **148**
*Bergenia cordifolia*, 31
  Evening Glow, 98
  Silver Light, 31, 43
*Beta cicla*, 123
betula, 25, 98, 132
*Betula albo-sinensis*, 98
  *caerulea-grandis*, 98
  *jacquemontii*, 98
  *pendula* Dalecarlica, 25
birch, 25, 98, 132

185

Town Gardens to Live In

bird splash, 132, **79, 80**
birds, 125, 132–3
blackberry, 125–6, 134
bluebell, 96
box, 56, 91, 151, 155, **92, 99**
bramble, ornamental, 96, 98, 131
brick
  paving, 56, 58–60, 64, 107, **58, 59**
  walls, 43, 71, 72, 92, 104, 136, 165–6, **44**
Brick Development Association, 165
British Bee-keepers' Association, 135, 184
broom, 93
*Brunnera macrophylla*, 96
*Buddleia alternifolia*, 32, 121, 131
  *davidii*, 135
  *fallowiana*, 32, 131
  *globosa*, 121
  *variabilis*, 131
bugle, 99
bulbs, 31, 56, 146, 153
butterflies, 131
buxus, 56, 91, 151, 155, **92, 99**
*Buxus balearica*, 93

calendula, 32, 131, 147, 153
*Caltha palustris*, 81, 89
camellia, 92, 151
*Camellia sasanqua*, 99, 100, 151
campanula, 96
*Campanula lactiflora*, 32
  *latifolia*, 32
  *poscharskyana*, 31, 48, 52, 93
car parking, 159–60
carrot, 122
*Caryopteris clandonensis*, 131, 135
catalpa, 98, **99**
catmint, 30
ceanothus, 93, 103
*Cedrus libani* Nana, 91
Cement and Concrete Association, 61, 167, 184
chadar, 86–8
*Chaenomeles speciosa*, 135
chard, Swiss, 123
cheiranthus, 32, 153
cherry, see *Prunus*

*Chimonanthus praecox*, 99
*Choisya ternata*, 151
chokeberry, 134
*Chrysanthemum maximum*, 32
cistus, 56, 111
clematis, 71, 72, 118, **74**
*Clematis integrifolia*, 32
  Lasurstern, 48
  *montana*, 69
*Clerodendron trichotomum*, **104**
cobbles, 61, 107, 117, 172–3, **62**
columbine, 30
compost, 18, 102, 137, 145–6, 163–4
concrete, 167–73
  paving, 60, 61–2, 64, 107, **57, 59**
  pools, 173–9
  raised beds, 173–4
  screens, 74–5, 92
cone flower, 131
*Convallaria majalis*, 96
coral berry, 135
*Cornus alba*, 98
  *a*. Elegantissima, 32, 40, **41**
  *canadensis*, 31
  *mas*, 100, 135
  *stolonifera*, 98
*Cortaderia selloana*, 93
*Cotinus coggygria*, 32
cotoneaster, 96, 98, 135
*Cotoneaster congestus*, 32
  *dammeri*, 31, 40, **41**
  *frigidus*, 42
  *glaucophyllus*, 92
  *horizontalis*, 93, 134, 158
  *h*. Variegatus, 32
  *salicifolia* Autumn Fire, **156**
  *s*. Rugosus, 92
  *simonsii*, 134
cotton lavender, 32, 151, 155
courgettes, 125
crab apple, 26, 126, 134
Craft Advisory Committee, 184
*Crambe cordifolia*, 32
cranesbill, see Geranium
*Crataegus monogyna*, 134
crinum, 153
crown imperial, 153
cucumber, 125
*Cupressus macrocarpa*, 69

# Index

currant, flowering, 96, 134, 135
  fruiting, 125
*Cyperus vegetus*, 89

dahlia, 32, 153
daphne, 96
*Daphne mezereum*, 100, 152
  *odora* Aureomarginata, 32, 100, 151
daphnia, 82, 131
day lily, 30, 32, 89, 96
dead nettle, 90, 96, 103
dianthus, 135
digitalis, 32, 90, 96
Disabled Living Foundation, 184
dogwood, see *Cornus*
doronicum, 96
*Doronicum cordifolia*, 31
*Dryopteris felix-mas*, 153
drying umbrella, 162, **163**
dustbins, 154, 157, 158, 161, **161**–2

*Echinacea purpurea*, 32, 131
echinops, 32, 131
*Echium* Blue Bedder, 32
eichhornia, 82, 88
elder, 93, 134
  golden, 93, **95**
eleagnus, 92
*Eleagnus angustifolia*, 32, 134
  *commutata*, 32
  *macrophylla*, 32
  *pungens* Maculata, 32, 93
  *umbellata*, 134
epimedium, 96, 158
*Epimedium* × *versicolor* Sulphureum, 48
eranthis, 100
*Erica carnea*, 32, 99, 100
  *darleyensis*, 100
*Eryngium planum*, 131
Escallonia, 106
*Escallonia* C. F. Ball, 121
  *iveyi*, 121
eschscholzia, 32
*Euonymus fortunei* Silver Queen, 32, 158
  *f.* Variegatus, 98–9
euphorbia, 155

*Euphorbia characias*, 32
  *wulfenii*, 32, 48
evening primrose, 31, 96

fastigiate trees, 26
*Fatsia japonica*, 48, 93, 151, 158, **157**
fences, 69, **70**
fennel, 30
ferns, 96, 144, 153, 158
fertilizers, 102, 159
fibreglass, 115, 139, 142, 147, **114**
firethorn, 96, 134
flax, New Zealand, 32, 93, **99**
foam flower, 31, 96
*Foeniculum vulgare*, 30
forget-me-not, 96
forsythia, 121
foxgloves, 32, 90, 96
fragaria, 96, 125
*Fritillaria imperialis*, 153
fuchsia, 96, 111, 152
*Fuchsia magellanica* Versicolor, 48, 152

gardener's garters, 89
*Garrya elliptica*, 93, 100
gazania, 152, **146**
gean, 25
*Genista hispanica*, 121
geranium, 90, 96; see also Pelargonium
*Geranium macrorrhizum*, 31, 52, 96
  Russell Prichard, 31
  *sanguineum lancastriense*, **97**
geum, 30
Gill, Eric, 13
globe artichoke, 122–3
globe thistle, 32, 131
goat's beard, 32
golden rod, 96, 135
Golders Green, garden at, **54**
gooseberry, 122, 128, **127**
gorse, 100, 121
grass, 55, 65
  seed, 65, 103
  soil requirements, 17
  turfing, 65

187

# Town Gardens to Live In

gravel, 63–4, 66–7, 107, **55**
greenhouses, 163
griselinia, 93
Gro-bags, 125, 142, **143**
ground cover, 31–2, 103, **104**
ground elder, 130
*Gunnera manicata*, 89
gypsophila, 32

*Hamamelis mollis*, 45, 96, 99, 100
Hampstead Heath, garden at, 39–40, **40–41**
Hardy Plant Society, 135
Hatfield, garden at, 93, **157**
hawthorn, 26, 134
hebe, 32, 103
*Hebe anomala*, 151
   *glaucophylla*, 32
   *parvifolia*, 151
   *pinguifolia* Pagei, 52
hedera, 55, 91, 93, 154, 161–2, **92**
*Hedera canariensis* Variegata, 158
   *colchica*, 32
   *c*. Variegata, 32, 39
   *helix*, 32
   *h*. Aureovariegata, 32
hedges, 69–71, 105–6, 107, 154, 161
helenium, 32
helianthemum, 56, 131
helianthus, 131
heliotrope, 153
hellebore, 96, 155
*Helleborus corsicus*, 100
   *niger*, 99, 100
   *n*. Macranthus, 99
   *orientalis*, 100
   *viridiis*, 100
*Helxine soleirolii*, **57, 97**
hemerocallis, 30, 32, 89, 96
*Heracleum mantegazzianum*, 103, 132, **102, 133**
herbaceous perennials, 27, 30, 146, 149
   ground cover, 31
   planting distances, 27, 30
   self-supporting, 30, 32
   soil requirements, 17
herbs, 15, 39, 45, 128, **127, 129**
*Hesperis matronalis*, 131

*Heuchera brizoides*, 96
   *tiarelloides* Bridget Bloom, 31
*Hippophae rhamnoides*, 32
hogweed, giant, 103, 132, **102, 133**
holly, 96, 106, 134
honeysuckle, see Lonicera
hornbeam, 26, 70–71, 106
hosta, 81, 89, 95, 96, 144, 159
*Hosta decorata*/Thomas Hogg, **94**
   *fortunei*, **83**
   *sieboldiana/glauca*, 153
   *undulata*, **97**
hurdles, wattle, 43, 68, 136, **44, 68, 164**
hyacinth, 146, 153
hydrangea, 96, 103, 144, 149
*Hydrangea macrophylla*, 152
   *paniculata*, **78**
   *petiolaris*, 48
hypericum, 96
*Hypericum calycinum*, 39, 43, 93, 155
   *forrestii*, 152

*Iberis sempervirens* Snowflake, 32
ilex, 96, 134
*Impatiens balsamina*, 153
Institute of Landscape Architects, 183
iris, 30
   bearded, 32, 48
*Iris histriodes major*, 147, 153
   *kaempferi*, 81, 89
   *laevigata*, 89, **88**
   *pseudacorus*, 89
   *sibirica*, 81
   *unguicularis/stylosa*, 100
ivy, see Hedera

Japanese garden design, 49, 52
Japanese wineberry, 125
*Jasminum nudiflorum*, 99, 100
Jekyll, Gertrude, 31, 123
juniper, 26
*Juniperus* Pfitzeriana, 91
   *sabina* Tamariscifolia, 91
   *virginiana* Grey Owl, 93

# Index

kalmia, 96
*Kerria japonica*, 96, **94**
kniphofia, 32, **104**

laburnum, 54
*Lamium galeobdolen*, 90, 96, 103
  *maculatum*, 96
laurel, see *Prunus*
*Laurus nobilis*, 48, 96, 151
lavender, 30, 32, 56, 131, 145, 151
*Lavandula spica* Munstead, 48
leek, 122, 123
Le Nôtre, 81
Lenten rose, 100
lettuce, 123-4
*Liatris spicata*, 131
lighting, 115, 141
  underwater, 84, 85
ligularia, 32, 96
*Ligularia dentata/Clivorum*, 30, 89
*Ligustrum vulgare* Sempervirens, 155; see also Privet
lilac, 48, 103, 131
lily, 31, 52, 111, 146, 150, 153, **145**
lily of the valley, 96
*Lippia citriodora*, 150
lobelia, 138
loganberry, 125
London pride, 31, 48, 96
lonicera, 131, 134
*Lonicera fragrantissima*, 99
  *japonica* Halliana, 69, 72, **73**
  *nitida*, 155
  *pileata*, 39, 56, **41**
  *standishii*, 100
loosestrife, 32
Loudon, J. C., 122
*Lysichitum americanum*, 89
*Lysimachia punctata*, 32

*Magnolia soulangeana*, 48
mahonia, 93, 96
*Mahonia bealei*, 31, 48
  *japonica*, 100
  *media*, 99
maple, see *Acer*
Marigold, 131
  pot, 32, 147, 153
marrow, 125, **127**

marsh marigold, 81, 89
mesembryanthemum, 141, 152
Milan, roof garden in, 140-42
Milton Keynes, housing at, **68, 69, 113, 158**
mimosa, 158, **157**
mind your own business, **57, 97**
Ministry of Agriculture, Food and Fisheries, 135
mock orange, 32, 96, 111
monarda, 32, 96
monk's hood, 32
Mono Concrete, 62, 74-5, 160, **148**
Monolok stones, 62
mowing stones, 49, 65, 103
Mughul emperors, 86
mullein, 30, 52
myosotis, 96

National Chrysanthemum Society, 184
National Dahlia Society, 184
nettles, 130-31
nicotiana, 32, 147, 153
nurseries, 10, 27, 182-3
nymphea, 82, 88

Oenothera, 96
*Oenothera missouriensis*, 31
*Olearia hastii*, 151
  *mollis*, 32
*Omphalodes verna*, 96
onion, 124-5
osier, 119
osmanthus, 96
*Osmunda regalis*, 153
*Oxalis acetosella*, 96, 130
oxygenating plants, 82, 89

*Pachysandra terminalis*, 32, 56, 96, 100
  *t*. Variegatus, 93
pampas grass, 93
paths, 22-4, 49, 51, 58, 130, 170-73, **23, 50, 58, 64**
pea, 122
  sweet, 124, 147
pear, silver-leaved, 51
  fruiting, 127, 142

189

Town Gardens to Live In

pelargonium, 31, 141, 149
  ivy-leaved, 149
  scented-leaved, 149–50
peony, herbaceous, 27, 31, 32, 96, **104**
perennials see Herbaceous perennials
pergolas, 111, 137, **20**, **110**, **112**
periwinkle, 48, 96, 154
perspective, 47, 49, 52
petunia, 31, 32, 131, 146, 147, 149, 152
*Phalaris arundinacea* Picta, 89
philadelphus, 96, 111
*Philadelphus coronarius* Variegatus, 32
phlox, 27, 32, 131
*Phlox drummondii*, 32, 152
*Phormium tenax*, 93, **99**
  t. Variegatum, 32
*Phyllitis scolopendrium*, 153
*Picea abies* Clanbrassiliana, 91
  *pungens* Glauca, 91
pieris, 96
*Pieris formosa forrestii*, 92, 151, **94**
  *japonica* Bert Chandler, 92
*Pinus mugo pumilio*, 91
plan-making, 24
plantain lily, see Hosta
plastics for pools, 81, 133, 166–7
polyanthus, 32, 146, 152
*Polygonatum multiflorum*, 89
polygonum, 96
*Polygonum baldschuanicum*, 69
  *vaccinifolium*, 96
*Pontederia cordata*, 89, **78**
pools, 77–83, 166, 167–9, 174–9
poppy, 30
  oriental, 32
  tree, 32
potentilla (shrubby), 32, 96
*Potentilla arbuscula* Beesii, 48
  Elizabeth, **156**
  *fruticosa* Abbotswood, 52
potting area, 163–4
primrose, 135
primula, 96
privet, 70, 105, 134, 154, 155, 161
pruning, 26

*Prunus avium*, 25
  *cistena*, 32
  *conradinae*, 100
  *davidiana*, 100
  *incisa* Praecox, 100
  *laurocerasus* Schipkaensis, 93
  *l. Zabeliana*, 93, 151
  *mume*, 100
  *serrula*, 25, **26**
  *subhirtella* Autumnalis, 26, 97, 99, **11**
pulmonaria, 96
pumps, 84–5, **80**
pyracantha, 96, 143
*Pyrus salicifolia* Pendula, 51

quince, ornamental, 135

radishes, 125
*Reader's Digest Complete Do-it-yourself Manual*, 11, 165
*Rhamnus frangula*, 131
*Rheum palmatum*, 81, 89, **95**
rhododendron, 15, 31, 32, 92, 96, 103, 145, 151
*Rhododendron arboreum*, 100
  Bluebird, 48
  *dauricum*, 100
  *mucronulatum*, 100
  *williamsianum*, 52
rhubarb, wild, 81, 89, **95**
*Ribes sanguineum*, 96, 134, 135
Riviera fencing, 111, 184
*Robinia pseudoacacia*, **90**
  *p.* Frisia, 26, 51
rock rose, 131
rodgersia, 96, **83**
*Romneya coulteri*, 32
rose, 15, 30, 31, 155, 158
  climbing roses, 69, 71, 106; Albertine, 118; Étoile de Hollande, 48; Sympathie, 48
  Felicia, 48
  floribunda roses, 48
  Nevada, 48
  *paulii*, **156**
  *rubiginosa* (sweetbriar), 131, 135
  *rubrifolia*, 131
  rugosa, 71, 121, 131

# Index

rose of Sharon, 39, 43, 93, 155
rosemary, 151
rowan, 25, 134
Royal Horticultural Society, 183
　Wisley gardens, **84, 88**
Royal National Rose Society, 184
Royal Society for the Protection of
　Birds, 7, 133, 184
rubus, 96
*Rubus biflorus*, 98
　*cockburnianus*, 98
　*odoratus*, 131
rudbeckia, 131
rue, 151, 158
russian vine, 69
Rye, garden at, 28–9


Sackville-West, V., 107
sage, 52, 151
　white, 32
salix, 132
*Salix alba* Britzensis, 98
　*caprea*, 135
　*chrysocoma*, 98
　*matsudana* Tortuosa, 26
　*purpurea*, 119
*Salvia officinalis*, 52, 151
*Sambucus nigra*, 134
　*n.* Aurea, 93, **95**
sand-pits, 15, 116–17
*Santolina chamaecyparissus*, 32, 151, 155
*Sarcocca humilis*, 48, 56, 96, 100
*Saxifraga umbrosa*, 31, 48, 96
*Scilla bifolia*, 100
*Scirpus zebrinus*, 89, **83**
screens, 71, 107, 136, **74, 110, 139**
sea buckthorn, 32
sea holly, 131
senecio, 96, 155
*Senecio greyi*, 32, 93, 151
　*laxifolius*, 32
setts, granite, 60, 64, 107, **61**
shrubs, 27, 31, 146
　ground cover, 31–2
　planting distances, 30
　soil requirements, 17

skimmia, 93, 96
*Skimmia japonica* Foremannii, 31, 151
*Smilacina racemosa*, 89
smoke bush, 32
snowberry, 96, 135
snowdrop, 31
solidago, 96, 135
Solomon's seal, 89
*Sorbus aucuparia*, 25, 134
　*discolor*, 25
　*hupehensis*, 25
　*megalocarpa*, 100
　*vilmorinii*, 25
spiraea, 96
*Spiraea* × *arguta* Bridal Wreath, **94**
squill, 100
*Stachys lanata*, **104**
staging, 35, **144**
stone paving, 62–4, 66–7, 107, **55, 57, 64**
stranvaesia, 96
strawberry, 122, 125
　alpine, 12, 96, 125
　pots, 125
sun, movement of, 15, **16**
sunflower, 131, 132
sweet corn, 123
sweet pea, 124, 147
sweet rocket, 131
sycamore, 15, **14**
symphoricarpos, 96, 135
syringa, 48, 103, 131


*tatami* system, 21
*Taxus baccata*, 54, 91–2, 106, 134
tellima, 96
terraces, 17, 35, **33–4, 36, 37**
thalictrum, 32
thuja, 69
*Thymus serpyllum*, 103, 131, **104**
*Tiarella cordifolia*, 31, 96
tiles
　asbestos, 137
　for pools, 80–81
　roofing, 75

191

timber
  decking, 64
  fences, 69
  screen, 75, **76**
tobacco, 32, 147, 153
tomato, 125, **143**
tradescantia, 96
tree of heaven, 51
trellis, 71–2, 161, **162**
tulip, 149, 153
*Tulipa kaufmanniana*, 31, 147, 153

*Ulex europaeus*, 100
Uni-Block paving, 62

*Verbascum bombyciferum*/Broussa 30
  Gainsborough, 52
  *vernale*, 52
verbena, 131
  lemon-scented, 150
veronica (shrubby), see Hebe
viburnum, 92, 96, 155, 159
*Viburnum bodnantse*, 99, 100
  *farreri*, 100
  *lantana*, 134
  *tinus*, 99, 100
  *tomentosum* Mariesii, **94**
*Vinca major*, 96, 154
  *minor*, 48, 96
vines, 128–9; see also *Vitis*

viola, 32, 152
violet, 135
*Vitis coignetiae*, 160, **159**

wall brackets, 35, **147**
wallflower, 32, 149, 153
walls, 43, 71–2, 74, 92, 95, 104, 165–6, **44**
water fleas, 82
water hyacinth, 82, 88
water lily, 81–3, 88
water snails, 82
watering, 137, 144–6
wattle hurdles, 43, 68, 136, **44, 68**
wayfaring tree, 134
weigela, 96
willow, see Salix
window-boxes, 138–9, 142, 158, **156**
winter aconite, 100
winter sweet, 99
Wisley gardens, **84, 88**
witch hazel, 45, 96, 99, 100
wood sorrel, 96, 130
woodruff, 39, 96
wrought iron screen, **76**

yew, 54, 91–2, 106, 134
*Yucca filamentosa*, 151
  *flaccida*, 93
zinnia, 32